David and Barbara Leeman have done it again. Their newest hymnal, *Hosanna in Excelsis*—a collection of carols and devotions for the Christmas season—unlocks the riches of the rescue mission we call the incarnation. Each hymn is accompanied by three sections: "Text" (on the background of both author and song), "Tune" (on the melody), and "As You Sing This Hymn" (practical application for thought and life). What a terrific resource to help families and churches lift their voices to the King in the manger, resting in the shadow of a cross.

MATT SMETHURST
Managing editor, The Gospel Coalition; author, *Before You Open Your Bible: Nine Heart Postures for Approaching God's Word*

In a day when the glorious message of Christmas and the incarnation of the Son of God are trivialized and commercialized, I can think of nothing more essential than this volume of theologically rich, devotionally inspiring, and biblically faithful hymns. What a wonderful gift this is not only for the individual believer but also for the church corporately. Thank you to the Leemans!

SAM STORMS
Lead Pastor of Preaching & Vision, Bridgeway Church, Oklahoma City, OK

Perhaps more families begin or restart family worship during the Christmas season than any other time of year. Whether this describes your family's intention, or you've been consistent in family worship for a long time, I want to commend *Hosanna in Excelsis* to you. It's a daily devotional that dovetails the biblical teaching upon which many seasonal hymns and carols are based with the lyrics and score of the songs themselves. So you'll learn some of the story behind each song and often about the hymn writer and/or composer, as well as discover biblical insights from the foundational passage for the song. Then, of course, you sing the song in worship of the One whose coming we celebrate at Christmas. Combine all that with the captivating calligraphy of Timothy Botts, and you have a family worship resource you'll enjoy year after year.

DONALD S. WHITNEY
Professor of biblical spirituality and associate dean at The Southern Baptist Theological Seminary, Louisville, KY; author of *Spiritual Disciplines for the Christian Life*, *Praying the Bible*, and *Family Worship*

One critical piece of Christmas being the most wonderful time of the year is the music. And if so in our increasingly secular society, how much more in the church. The angels sang. Mary sang. The magi bowed in worship. The shepherds shared their joy, and all who heard it wondered at what the shepherds told them. And we too sing. The coming of God Himself in human flesh is too great to only keep silent. We must soon enough lift our voices, and as our praises go up, they complete our joy that Christ came down to dwell among us. I look forward to making this volume my annual reference for enjoying my favorite Christmas hymns all the more, and learning some new ones as well.

DAVID MATHIS
Executive editor, desiringGod.org; pastor, Cities Church, St. Paul, Minnesota; author, *The Christmas We Didn't Expect*

The Leemans have done it again! We have recommended their Student Hymnal in our curriculum for several years, and now I am happy to be able to answer our members when they ask if we can recommend any resources specifically for the Christmas season from Advent through Epiphany. The collection includes both well-loved and new-to-me hymns, along with fascinating information about the writers and composers. The Leemans' piano accompaniment recordings are beautiful enough to listen to even when we are not singing. This would be such a welcome addition to any family music library.

JEN SPENCER
Program Director, Charlotte Mason's Alveary

Effectively compiled, this inspiring, informative collection of Christmas hymns is an essential resource, rejoicing the hearts of those who envision themselves as participants in the incarnation narrative. Emphasizing the church year, *Hosanna in Excelsis* invigorates the inner spirit, bringing expectation, fulfillment, and light to our darkened world.

LOREN WIEBE
Emeritus Professor of Music, Biola University, La Mirada, CA

At Christmas why do we sing the songs we sing, often over and over? Perhaps we need to ask, "Why did they write the songs they wrote?" Once again David and Barbara Leeman have given us a gift by taking us behind the scenes of these marvelous Christmas hymns and showing us devotionally how these hymns and carols came together to bring God glory. With elegant and precise explanation, this hymnal enlightens the way I celebrate and marvel in the majesty and mystery of the Incarnation. This hymnal has beautifully informed how my family and my church worship from Advent through Epiphany. God has used this hymnal to transform the way I eagerly approach the season of Advent and how I expectantly wait for the second advent—it will you too.

MARK DAVIS
Senior Pastor, Park Cities Presbyterian Church, Dallas, TX

One of the most encouraging trends of recent years is the recommitment of God's people to family worship. *Hosanna in Excelsis* is ideal for family devotions during the Christmas season, providing the stories behind beloved carols, while presenting the music in a lovely form. What a treat to families to read these stories and sing these songs during the Christmas season! *Hosanna in Excelsis* will also be valuable to pastors in connecting God's people to our heritage of faith in celebrating Jesus' birth. David and Barbara Leeman have opened their hearts and poured forth the beauty of God's gift of His Son. Their wonderful book will inspire hearts and inform minds, prompting to our Savior the songs of joy that His coming deserves.

RICHARD D. PHILLIPS
Senior Minister, Second Presbyterian Church, Greenville, SC

Hymns & Devotions
for the Christmas Season

David & Barbara Leeman

Music Engraving, David Leeman
Titles Calligraphy, Timothy Botts

MOODY PUBLISHERS
CHICAGO

Unless otherwise indicated, Scripture quotations are from The ESV® Bible (The Holy Bible, English Standard Version®), copyright © 2001 by Crossway, a publishing ministry of Good News Publishers. Used by permission. All rights reserved.

Scripture quotations marked (NIV) are taken from the Holy Bible, New International Version®, NIV®. Copyright © 1973, 1978, 1984, 2011 by Biblica, Inc.™ Used by permission of Zondervan. All rights reserved worldwide. www.zondervan.com. The "NIV" and "New International Version" are trademarks registered in the United States Patent and Trademark Office by Biblica, Inc.™

Scripture quotations marked KJV are taken from the King James Version.

All emphasis in Scripture has been added.

Published in association with the literary agency of Wolgemuth and Associates.

This book was previously self-published in 2018. Some of the text and tune backgrounds were originally self-published in a book titled *Hosanna, Loud Hosannas, a Student Hymnal* (2014).

Edited by Amanda Cleary Eastep
Interior Design: Erik M. Peterson
Cover art and design by Stephen Crotts

All websites and phone numbers listed herein are accurate at the time of publication but may change in the future or cease to exist. The listing of website references and resources does not imply publisher endorsement of the site's entire contents. Groups and organizations are listed for informational purposes, and listing does not imply publisher endorsement of their activities.

Library of Congress Cataloging-in-Publication Data

Names: Leeman, David, author. | Leeman, Barbara, author.
Title: Hosanna in excelsis : hymns and devotions for the Christmas season /
   David and Barbara Leeman ; music engraving, David Leeman, titles
   calligraphy, Timothy Botts.
Description: Chicago : Moody Publishers, 2020. | Includes bibliographical
   references. | Summary: "Celebrate the coming of Christ by immersing
   yourself in the legacy of music that truly honors the Christmas season.
   Hosanna in Excelsis is a devotional that couples the lyrics and score of
   a new hymn daily with a devotional message about the music's biblical
   and spiritual truths"-- Provided by publisher.
Identifiers: LCCN 2020020753 (print) | LCCN 2020020754 (ebook) | ISBN
   9780802421982 (hardcover) | ISBN 9780802498854 (ebook)
Subjects: LCSH: Advent hymns--History and criticism. | Christmas
   music--History and criticism. | Advent--Prayers and devotions. |
   Christmas--Prayers and devotions. | Advent hymns. | Christmas music.
Classification: LCC ML3270 .L44 2020 (print) | LCC ML3270 (ebook) | DDC
   781.723--dc23
LC record available at https://lccn.loc.gov/2020020753
LC ebook record available at https://lccn.loc.gov/2020020754

Originally delivered by fleets of horse-drawn wagons, the affordable paperbacks from D. L. Moody's publishing house resourced the church and served everyday people. Now, after more than 125 years of publishing and ministry, Moody Publishers' mission remains the same—even if our delivery systems have changed a bit. For more information on other books (and resources) created from a biblical perspective, go to www.moodypublishers.com or write to:

Moody Publishers
820 N. LaSalle Boulevard
Chicago, IL 60610

1 3 5 7 9 10 8 6 4 2

Printed in the United States of America

To our own dear children, grandchildren,
and all other children who love Christmas.

Ding, Dong! Merrily on high,
in heav'n the bells are ringing!
Ding, Dong! Verily the sky
is riv'n with angel singing!
Gloria! Hosanna in Excelsis!

Contents

HYMNS OF EPIPHANY

Foreword

The incarnation, God becoming man, was heralded by angels singing a simple song even lowly, frightened shepherds could understand. In the twenty centuries since that miraculous birth, the song has never been silent: *Peace on earth—Joy—Bethlehem—The Child—A star—The Magi*. Wherever Christ is known—in every generation, every culture, every social class—the seasons of Advent, Christmas, and Epiphany resound with carols. From childhood to old age we sing those simple, heartfelt tunes regaling God's Precious Gift, and in singing, each time, we overflow with wonder.

It is right (and wonderful) that David and Barbara Leeman have once again offered their hearts, along with their musical gifts, in this most remarkable collection, *Hosanna in Excelsis*. More than an accumulation of carols, it is *history*, reclaiming expressions of joy and delight from the earliest carols through the centuries to our own day. It is *personal*, recounting the stories, the people, and the inspirations behind the music. It is *instructive*, pointing our hearts toward singing with understanding, gratitude, and delight. And it is *scriptural*, giving credence through God's Word to the joys we so fervently express. Earth and heaven, body and soul, are joined. The day will come when we sing with the angels: "The kingdom of this world is become the Kingdom of our Lord and of His Christ."[1] Even as we wait expectantly, incarnation is that promise carrying us to our eternal reward. Therefore, in joy and thanksgiving, we sing: *Hosanna in Excelsis!*

GREGORY S. ATHNOS
Emeritus Professor of Music
North Park University, Chicago, Illinois

Preface

Stop and think about it. Have you ever heard of songs being written to commemorate a baby's birth? Any songs about the birth of Alexander the Great, Napoleon, or Gandhi? When a modern royal has a baby, it makes the news for a few days, but there are no songs about that baby. Now imagine this: What if you did not know that hundreds, perhaps thousands, of songs have been written about the birth of Jesus? Then someone told you this was so. Would you be curious to know why?

Obviously, Jesus was no ordinary baby. But His birth in an obscure Middle Eastern village in poorest of circumstances was not what you might expect of one for whom songs are written. These are songs that have been sung over and over for millennia and that are a part of almost every language and culture. Perhaps this is something important for you to discover and know.

This book is only a small collection of those songs. But it is representative of the best that have prevailed over time and have become a major part of our celebration of Christ's birth, known as Christmas. Luke 2:19 says that after the visit by the shepherds, Jesus' mother, Mary, "treasured up all these things, pondering them in her heart." Most of us are a lot better at *doing* than *pondering*. This book is for both pondering and doing (singing). These songs are like a picture album of the story of our blessed Lord Jesus. From them, you can treasure the amazing events that surround His birth. You can ponder them as each hymn writer unfolds a slightly different picture or perspective. You can more deeply think about what they mean to you today than you can in the midst of a service or concert of Christmas music.

You can read all the forty-three songs in one or two sittings. Or you can focus on one hymn per day, spending ten minutes being fed by the testimonies of many Christian hymn writers. This practice will ensure these songs and their stories ring deeply in your heart of affection for the incarnate Son of God. Each day you or your family can choose a Christmas hymn to sing together and ponder the story.

There are dozens of Advent-Christmas devotional books available to believers; however, in this collection, forty-three authors share their spiritual view of Christmas—simple, brief, but powerful words about a birth and the surrounding circumstances.

Think about how many Christmas hymns you know beyond the first stanza. Here, you may learn all the stanzas. You'll find some new, or less familiar, hymns; however, all the Christmas hymns in this book are songs that every Christian should know and sing. Each hymn has been chosen for its singability and depth of meaning. A few may have poetic sentimentality more than strict biblical accuracy, but for centuries they have comprised our Christmas canon of songs.

This collection covers the church or Christian calendar for this season. Advent begins four Sundays before Christmas and includes the days between the fourth Sunday and Christmas Day. Therefore, you can observe the Advent season for anywhere from twenty-two to twenty-eight days. For that reason, the dates listed for each hymn cover the longest potential Advent season of any year's calendar. (So some years you will have more devotionals than the season measures.) Christmas and Christmastide continue until January 6, the twelfth day of Christmas, or Epiphany. The hymns that are obviously Advent, Nativity, or Epiphany texts, however, will overlap the calendar designations. What we call Christmas in general encompasses a forty-three-day-long observation and celebration.

Since knowing about the author of a book generally helps you understand the book, brief biographies of the authors and composers have been included to place their poetic and melodic testimony in the time and circumstances of their lives. The author of a hymn's words was not always the composer of the music. The melodies often have their own title, specified through ALL CAPS.

Following each biography is a brief devotional on the hymn text called, "As you sing this hymn." These sections aren't titled "as you *read* this hymn" but "as you *sing*" because Scripture repeatedly says we should *sing* to the Lord.

Sing if you are alone or with others. Sing even if you feel like you do not sing well. To make this easier for you and your family, the hymns have been recorded in two formats: with singers, and with piano only, so you can sing along. The recording features two adults and three children—like the sound of a family. You can purchase this recording on most streaming services, such as Spotify or iTunes, or you can purchase the songs on other user-friendly formats at hosannahymnals.com. A book containing the piano arrangements for all the hymns on the recording is also available. Sing along during your family devotional time! Sing when you're preparing a meal! Sing along on a car trip!

Are these Christmas *hymns* or Christmas *carols*? Yes. They are both! As *hymns*, they are songs of the story and the theology of the incarnation—the Son of God becoming man. They also are *carols* of joy, celebration, and even dance— one definition of a carol.[2] Both words will be used interchangeably. These are the testimonies and convictions of saints through seventeen centuries of worship—from the fourth century through the twenty-first century. They cross most denominational and generational barriers. They answer the ubiquitous questions of what, who, when, and why. They quote the Bible and, at times, also interpret it for us. But most of all, they provide rich and beautiful words for our worship of the God who sent His Son to earth.

Our prayer is that this book will serve as an enduring and inspiring gift from parents to children or family and friends, to those who are on your Christmas card list, or from a church to its members. In giving this book away, you are sharing great treasures you love as well as treasures you have just discovered. The hymns themselves are timeless gifts that began in the heart of someone who was devoted to Christ and wrote down that conviction in beautiful poetry. Now these gifts are being passed on through us to generations yet unborn. May God bless your Advent, Christmas, and Epiphany seasons.

ADVENT

THE PRACTICE OF OBSERVING the church year is not known by all Christians. The terms Advent, Christmas, Epiphany, Lent, and Easter are not in the Bible. But Christians began following the Church Year—also called the Christian Year— perhaps as far back as the fifth century. The practice is a way to regularly focus our hearts on aspects of God's story, specifically in the life of Jesus Christ.

The Church Year begins with Advent, a word from a version of the Latin word that means "coming." Of course, what is coming is our celebration of the birth date of Jesus. Just as any home and family that is expecting a newborn will prepare for the birth, so Christians prepare for Christmas. Israel spent thousands of years in perpetual Advent, waiting for the promised Messiah. But now He has come!

How do we today prepare during the season of Advent? Some people keep Advent calendars for daily thoughts or activities. Others use Advent wreaths with four to five candles. A single candle is lit each Sunday of Advent until Christmas Eve, when a center candle may be lit.

While the season of Advent prepares us for December 25, it does more than that. It helps us to anticipate Christ's future return—His second coming. We might even say there are four kinds of Advent: the historical time preceding Jesus' birth in Bethlehem; the Advent days of this year and this year's celebration; remembering the period of our personal lives before we came to know Jesus personally as Savior and Lord; and the "Second Advent" that we are in now, awaiting Christ's return to rule this earth.

One writer wisely observed: "One of the essential paradoxes of Advent: that while we wait for God, we are with God all along. That while we need to be reassured of God's arrival, or the arrival of our homecoming, we are already at home."[3]

So if Christ has already come and "we are with God all along," why should we celebrate a season of Advent? We prepare to once again celebrate His birthday while understanding He continually comes to us who are His children. His first coming is the foundation of our faith. While "we are already home," His promise to come again and take us to our eternal home is the source of our hope. May these hymns guide you into these wonderful truths and give you profound words for your Advent worship.

WHAT SWEETER MUSIC CAN WE BRING
Than a carol for to sing
The birth of this our heavenly King?
Awake the voice! awake the string!

. . . .

Dark and dull night, fly hence away,
And give the honour to this day,
That sees December turn'd to May.

. . . .

Why does the chilling winter's morn
Smile like a field beset with corn?
Or smell like to a mead new shorn,
Thus, on the sudden?

Come and see
The cause, why things thus fragrant be:
'Tis He is born, whose quick'ning birth
Gives life and lustre, public mirth,
To heaven and the under-earth.

We see Him come, and know Him ours,
Who, with His sunshine and His showers,
Turns all the patient ground to flowers.

The darling of the world is come,
And fit it is we find a room
To welcome Him.

The nobler part
Of all the house here is the heart,

Which we will give Him; and bequeath
This holly and this ivy wreath,
To do Him honour; who's our King,
And Lord of all this revelling.

ROBERT HERRICK (1591–1674)[4]

TEXT: Johannes G. Olearius   ‖   b. September 17, 1611
Translated, Catherine Winkworth ‖ d. April 24, 1684

Johannes Olearius was a philosophy professor at the University of Wittenberg, Halle, Germany, but he is primarily remembered for his hymn writing. Three hundred and two of his hymns were included in one of the most important German hymnals of the 1600s, *Geistliche Singe-Kunst*. One of the hymns was the basis for "Cantata 129" by Johann Sebastian Bach.

TUNE: Louis Bourgeois   ‖   b. 1510, Paris, France
‖ d. 1561, Paris, France

Louis Bourgeois, a French composer, is famous for his Psalm tunes and was one of the three primary composers of the famous Genevan Psalter. OLD HUNDREDTH, the melody to which we sing "The Doxology," is commonly attributed to him. We may think people feel strongly about changes in church music today, but the local church authorities had Bourgeois sent to prison in 1551 for replacing the tunes of some well-known psalms "without a license."[5] John Calvin intervened and obtained his release. Still, controversy remained as people did not want to learn new tunes. The town council ordered the burning of Bourgeois' instructions to singers, declaring they were confusing. GENEVAN 42 was originally written for a setting of Psalm 42. When the tune is sung at a brisk tempo, its irregular meter is rollicking and joyful as befits the text.

As you sing this hymn . . . you are singing Isaiah 40:1, 3, printed under the hymn title. Isaiah records many tumultuous years for Israel. Some kings in this prophet's day were righteous, some were unrighteous. But throughout, the book is punctuated with God's promises of a Messiah who would bring comfort. Read this promise in #4 of the "Christmas in the Bible" section.

How Israel longed for comfort! Isaiah used the word "comfort" seven times to describe God's kindness to Israel. Pastor Mark Dever says of Isaiah, "The book is far more about God's tenacious concern in judgment and love for his people than his people's love for him . . . whether that love is expressed through his judgment upon their evil or through his promises of future deliverance."[6] Pastor Scotty Smith calls the words of Isaiah a description of "Advent arms."[7] "He gathers the lambs in His arms and carries them close to His heart" (40:11). What could be more comforting?

The Hebrew word for comfort can also be translated "repent."[8] At its root is the idea of breathing deeply or sighing, perhaps a sorrowful sigh for sin or a breath of relief when comfort is found. Significantly, Isaiah's words are in the present tense. The Israelites did not have to wait until Jesus was born to know comfort through repentance. God would have mercy on them then. Today, too, we do not have to wait for the return of Christ to find comfort. Comfort begins with our repentance, which means turning from sin. By repentance, we become reconciled with God, and that is where we find comfort and peace. Advent is a time for repentance, a time to sweep out the dirt and get ready for the coming Guest. Stanza four entreats, "Let your hearts be true and humble" as you prepare for Christmas. The promise of comfort is assured, for "God's word is never broken."

Comfort, comfort my people, says your God. . . . A voice
cries: "In the wilderness prepare the way of the LORD;
make straight in the desert a highway for our God.

ISAIAH 40:1, 3

GENEVAN 42
Text: Johannes G. Olearius; Tr. Catherine Winkworth
Music: Louis Bourgeois

1. "Com - fort,com - fort now My peo - ple;   tell   of peace!" so says our   God.
2. Yea,   her sins   our God will par - don,   blot - ting out   each dark mis - deed:
3. For   the her - ald's voice is cry - ing   in   the des - ert far   and   near,
4. Straight shall be   what long was crook - ed,   and   the rough - er plac - es   plain!

Com - fort those who sit in dark - ness   mourn - ing un - der sor - row's load.
All   that well de-served His an - ger   He   no more will see   or   heed.
call - ing us   to true re-pent - ance   since the King - dom now   is   here.
Let   your hearts be true and hum - ble,   as   be - fits His ho - ly   reign!

To   God's peo - ple now pro-claim   that   God's par - don waits for them!
She   has suf - fered man-y a   day,   now   her griefs have passed a - way;
Oh,   that warn - ing cry o - bey!   Now   pre-pare   for God a - way!
For   the glo - ry of the Lord   now   on earth   is shed a -broad,

Tell   them that their war is o - ver;   God   will reign in peace for- ev - er!
God will change her pin -ing sad - ness   in - to ev - er spring-ing glad - ness!
Let   the val - leys rise to meet Him,   and   the hills bow down to greet_ Him.
and   all flesh shall see the to - ken   that God's word is nev - er bro - ken.

November 26   On Jordan's Bank the Baptist's Cry

TEXT: Charles Coffin ‖ b. October 4, 1676
d. June 20, 1749

Carolo (Charles) Coffin was born in Buzancy, France. He showed much promise as a child, and by age thirty-six, he became the principal of the College at Beauvais, and later the Rector of the University of Paris. But Coffin is most remembered for his hymns—over ninety can be found with English translations. This hymn may not be well-known, yet it is printed in 145 modern hymnals. Englishman John Chandler translated the original text in Latin in the nineteenth century.

A man of strong convictions, Coffin appealed against the positions of the Pope's 1713 edict on doctrine, called the *Constitution Unigenitus,* condemning a French movement called Jansenism that sought to reform the church's understanding of grace. As a result, the Catholic Church refused to grant him a Christian burial. But like Martin Luther, Coffin stood firm on the principles of God's Word. No wonder he wrote in stanza four the prayer, "let Your light restore earth's own true loveliness once more."

TUNE: Trier manuscript, 15th c. ‖ b. February 15, 1571
Adapted, Michael Praetorius   d. February 15, 1621

Michael Praetorius was a highly esteemed German composer, organist, and teacher. He is known for the development of musical forms based on Protestant hymns. His works include a collection of 1,200 chorales and song arrangements for the Lutheran church. Another of his Christmas hymns in this book is "Lo, How a Rose E'er Blooming."

As you sing this hymn . . . you are singing of what today might be called the prequel to the Christmas story. This was the ministry that God gave to John the Baptist. Refresh your memory of this amazing story by reading "Christmas in the Bible," #18 and 19.

Elizabeth, the mother of John the Baptist, and Mary, the mother of Jesus, were cousins and pregnant at the same time. Both births were miraculous, and John's parents are greatly honored in the story in Luke 1:57–80. John's words to Israel are also words to us today. Christ is coming—prepare the way in your hearts.

Stanza two in "On Jordan's Bank the Baptist's Cry" guides us to prepare through repentance. Stanzas three and four acknowledge our salvation as a gift of His grace, without which we are as doomed as flowers—bright for a season, but then gone. The world's current darkness cannot be transformed by political policies or social programs. It can only be restored by His light that entered our world with Jesus' coming. The final stanza is a doxology to the Trinity, leading us to give praise for this wondrous story of God's rescue.

Do you think of repentance as part of your Christmas preparation? Typically, we prepare for Christmas through decorating, gift buying, special cooking, traveling, and attending parties. But John the Baptist reminds us that Christmas preparation must begin with a personal inventory of our lives. Consider your sin—both the bad you've done and the good you've left undone. Then bring them to God in confession. No, you don't clean yourself up before you come to God. You bring the dirt to God, acknowledging it and asking Him to make you clean. Tell Him you need forgiveness as you prepare today for celebrating the Nativity.

On Jordan's Bank the Baptist's Cry

*These things took place in Bethany across the Jordan,
where John was baptizing.*

JOHN 1:28

PUER NOBIS
Text: Charles Coffin, Tr. John Chandler
Music: Trier Manuscript, adapt. Michael Praetorius

1. On Jor - dan's bank the Bap - tist's cry
2. Let ev - ery heart be cleansed from sin,
3. For You are our sal - va - tion, Lord,
4. To heal the sick, stretch out Your hand,
5. To You, O Christ, all prais - es be,

an - nounc - es that___ the Lord is nigh:
make straight the way___ for God with - in,
our re - fuge and___ our great re - ward;
and make the fal - len sin - ner stand;
Whose ad - vent sets___ Your peo - ple free;

a - wake and lis - ten for he brings
and so pre - pare to be the home
with - out Your grace we waste a - way
shine out, and let Your light re - store
Whom with the Fa - ther we a - dore

glad tid - ings of the King of kings.
where such a might - y guest may come.
like flowers that with - er and de - cay.
earth's own true love - li - ness once more.
and Ho - ly Spir - it ev - er - more.

TEXT: Jane Parker Huber ‖ b. October 24, 1926, Tsinan (now Jinan), China
d. November 17, 2008, Hanover, Indiana

Jane Parker Huber was born in China to missionary parents. They returned to America in 1929 when her father was appointed the president of Hanover College. Jane graduated from Hanover in 1948, married a pastor, and moved to Indiana. It wasn't until 1976 that she began writing hymns, but by 1996 she had over 125 hymns published. Jane was awarded a Doctor of Humane Letters in 1988 by Hanover College. In this hymn, Huber pictures the state of mind of what was probably a very early teenage girl who receives the shocking and almost incomprehensible news that she will be the mother of the Messiah. And though the centuries-long national prayer for a Messiah was the prayer of every Jew, no doubt many women dreamed of having the unparalleled honor of being the mother of the Messiah.

TUNE: Traditional English Folk Tune ‖ b. October 12, 1872, Gloucestershire, England
Arranged, Ralph Vaughan Williams ‖ d. August 26, 1958, London, England

It is unlikely that Jane Parker Huber used this tune for her text. But in this collection, it seemed appropriate and unifying to use the same tune for the parallel texts that speak of Mary and Joseph. KINGSFOLD is an ancient tune that some scholars think goes back to the Middle Ages and was used with a variety of texts in both England and Ireland. It was first published in 1893. The composer Ralph Vaughan Williams arranged it for a setting of another text by Horatius Bonar named, "I Heard the Voice of Jesus Say." This tune is unusual as it sounds both minor and major, but is likely based on one of the seven modal keys from early music. Modal keys use different arrangements of whole and half steps than major or minor.

As you sing this hymn . . . you come alongside someone who was crucial to the Christmas story—Jesus' mother, Mary. The opening stanza reveals a paradox that this highest honor would also come to enormous grief. Read and meditate on the story from "Christmas in the Bible," #9–21.

You will see that Mary's humility is remarkable. She did not understand how she could be pregnant before marriage, but she simply responds to the angel's explanation with these words: "I am the servant of the Lord; let it be to me according to your word" (Luke 1:38). There is no argument or reluctance.

Mary's prayer that follows is sometimes called the *Magnificat,* based on the third word in her prayer, "My soul magnifies the Lord" (v. 46). It is incredible that such a young, probably illiterate, peasant girl understood the ways of God as described in her song. Few others write with such clear and insightful theology of the nature of God.

Why should we sing a hymn—a Christmas carol—about Mary? Do we offer it as a form of worship of Mary—a type of veneration or honoring of a "saint"? No. We know that Mary, like all of us, needed a Savior. In her prayer, she says, "he has looked on the humble estate of his servant" (v. 48). Then she proclaims, "my spirit rejoices in God my Savior" (v. 47b) and "he who is mighty has done great things for me" (v. 49). We do not come to Mary as a means of reaching her Son. Rather, we learn from her obedience and devotion. Her song becomes our song of praise. As the carol says, "we join the song that Mary sings."

For Ages Women Hoped and Prayed 3

The angel said to her, ". . . You will conceive
in your womb and bear a son, and you shall call
his name Jesus." . . . And Mary said, "Behold,
I am the servant of the Lord; let it be to me
according to your word."

LUKE 1:30–31, 38

KINGSFOLD
Text: Jane Parker Huber
Music: Traditional English Melody; Arr. Ralph Vaughan Williams

1. For_ ag - es wom-en hoped and prayed to_ bear the A- noint-ed One,
2. Young Ma - ry did not think to hope for_ mir - a - cles_ of birth,
3. Our hearts re-joice as Ma - ry's song be - comes our hymn of praise.

both Is-rael's Sav - ior and the world's, the_ new day's shin - ing Sun.
and_ God chose her to be the one to_ make Christ's home on earth.
For_ Christ has come, Em - man - u - el! to_ claim our years and days.

Did_ they not know? Did they not guess what pain would then be theirs,
So_ Ma - ry sang her heart-felt praise of God who sets things straight;
Both pres-ent now and com-ing still, ac -com -plished fact and dream,

if_ God's A- noint-ed_ graced their home in_ an-swer to_ their prayers?
the_ might-y fall,_ the_ weak are raised, the_ hun-gry fill_ their plate.
we_ join the song that_ Ma - ry sings, an_ earth-ly, heaven-ly theme.

TEXT: Thomas H. Troeger ‖ b. 1945

Thomas Troeger is ordained in both the Episcopal and the Presbyterian churches and is professor emeritus at Yale Divinity School. A poet of many hymns and a flutist, he has served as the national chaplain of the American Guild of Organists. Troeger has written twenty books on hymnody and worship, preaching, and poetry, including *Wonder Reborn: Preaching on Hymns, Music, and Poetry*. The craftsmanship of a professional poet is clearly evident in this rare accounting of the earthly father of Jesus. John Greenleaf Whittier once said, "A good hymn is the best use to which poetry can be devoted."⁹

TUNE: Traditional English Folk Tune ‖ b. October 12, 1872, Gloucestershire, England
Arranged, Ralph Vaughan Williams ‖ d. August 26, 1958, London, England

Ralph Vaughan Williams started collecting folk songs in 1903 by going into the English countryside, noting down, and transcribing songs traditionally sung in various locations. He named this tune KINGSFOLD and used it in hymnody. Many of these tunes are also found throughout his nine symphonies and hundreds of other compositions. To connect the two hymn texts about Mary and Joseph, we chose to employ the same tune for both carols.

As you sing this hymn . . . you are singing one of the only Christmas hymns that mentions Joseph, the earthly father of Jesus. We know little about Joseph. We know he was a carpenter because Matthew and Mark both refer to the amazement people had at Jesus' wisdom and teaching when He was "a carpenter's son." Read "Christmas in the Bible," #9–12, to be reminded of Joseph's extraordinary trust and obedience at the angel's words.

Scripture testifies that Joseph was devoted to Mary and was concerned for her comfort, privacy, and safety. "Because Joseph her husband was faithful to the law, and yet did not want to expose her to public disgrace, he had in mind to divorce her quietly" (Matt. 1:19 NIV). Once an angel appears and explains it to him, there is no indication of doubt in Joseph's mind that this newborn was sent by God and was the Son of God: "He did what the angel of the Lord had commanded him" (v. 24 NIV). The poet's imagination then links his care for Mary to his handling of the newborn infant.

The prophet Isaiah had already revealed Immanuel as a name for this baby, and Matthew defines that name as "God with us" (v. 23). Yet the angel told Joseph the child should have a second name: Jesus, which means, "God saves." J. C. Ryle helped us understand the significance of the name when he wrote, "He, who is the King of kings and the Lord of lords, might lawfully have taken some more high-sounding title. But He does not do so. The rulers of this world have often called themselves great, conquerors, bold, magnificent, and the like. The Son of God is content to call Himself, Savior."¹⁰

What awful irony that the tools of Joseph's profession were used to crucify his son. We too can use the tools and skills God gives us for good or evil. In the final line, Troeger implores us to hold the child and be charged with faith. Let us be obedient like Joseph, even if we don't understand a call from God.

The Hands That First Held Mary's Child 4

When Joseph woke up,
he did what the angel of the Lord had commanded him
and took Mary home as his wife.

MATTHEW 1:24 NIV

KINGSFOLD
Text: Thomas H. Troeger
Music: Traditional English melody; Arr. Ralph Vaughan Williams

1. The_ hands that first held Ma-ry's child were hard from work-ing wood,
2. When Jo-seph mar-veled at the size of__ that small breath-ing frame,
3. "This child shall be Em-man-u-el, not__ God up-on__ the throne,
4. The_ tools which Jo-seph laid a-side a____ mob would lat-er lift

from__ boards they sawed and planed and filed and__ splin-ters they_ with-stood.
and__ gazed up-on those bright new eyes and__ spoke the in-fant's name,
but__ God with us, Em-man-u-el, as__ close as blood and bone."
and__ use with an-ger, fear, and pride to__ cru-ci-fy__God's gift.

This_ day they gripped no tool of steel, they drove no ir-on nail,
the_ an-gel's words he once had dreamed poured down from heav-en's height,
The_ tin-y form in Jo-seph's palms con-firmed what he had heard,
Let_ us, O Lord, not on-ly hold the childwho's born to-day,

but_ crad-led from the_ head to heel our_ Lord, new-born_ and frail.
and_ like the host of_ stars that beamed blessed earth with wel-come light.
and_ from his heart_ rose hymns and psalms for_ heav-en's hu-man word.
but_charged with faith may we be bold to_ fol-low in_ His way.

November 29   O Come, O Come, Emmanuel

TEXT: Latin antiphon
Translated, John Mason Neale, 1710   ‖   12th c. Latin hymn

An "antiphon" is a song that is sung back and forth between two groups with a call and response. "Anti" means opposite; "phon" means voice or sound. In the church of the Middle Ages, worshipers would sing seven antiphons the week before Christmas, all beginning with "O Come." They were called the "Great O's." Each would use an Old Testament name for the coming Messiah. Five of these names are:

Immanuel (God with us)	Isaiah 7:14
Rod of Jesse (David's offspring)	Isaiah 11:1, 10
Dayspring (Morning Star)	Numbers 24:17
Key of David	Isaiah 22:22
Desire of Nations	Haggai 2:7

By the twelfth century, these antiphons became the Latin Hymn, sung as one song. Each verse asks the coming Messiah to ransom, save, cheer, guide, and bring peace to the world. Following these "calls," the congregation "responds," knowing by faith that these requests will be heard and answered.

TUNE: Plainsong, 13th c.   ‖

The tune name, VENI EMMANUEL, is Latin for "Come, Emmanuel." It is based on the Latin plainsongs (or chants) of the thirteenth century and first appears in *Hymnal Noted, Part II* (London, 1854) arranged by Thomas Helmore. Try to sing the first stanza in Latin (similar to Spanish) to connect more viscerally with the early church.

As you sing this hymn . . . you are offering a prayer similar to the prayer that Israel prayed for centuries: delivery from civil oppressors such as Babylon and Rome. We pray to be released from this world's oppressions, but especially the oppression of sin and death. Similarly, the Old Testament prophets spoke of a day when God would ransom Israel from death and captivity. Wonderfully, this is the work Jesus came to do—to offer His life as a ransom for the sins of many (Matt. 20:28). Consider the definition of the word "ransom," prominent in the first stanza of the hymn.

A person is kidnapped, and often the kidnappers demand a ransom to be paid. Death makes just such a demand for payment on us. Unlike kidnappers, however, death's demand is just. We deserve to die for our sin (see Rom. 6:23). The good news of the gospel is that Jesus pays this ransom for all who repent and believe.

There is much sorrow in this world. John Piper wrote, "It is a wonderful thing that there are Christmas carols that are written for the real world of sorrowful joy."[11] That's what Christ's ransom produces in us—sorrowful joy. So we exclaim, "Rejoice! Rejoice!" What greater joy could we know than, in this evil world, God is with us? The ransom has been paid. His coming cheers us, closing the path to misery and making safe the way to our heavenly home. If you are experiencing sorrow this Christmas, may this hymn lift those burdens and give you joy.

O Come, O Come, Emmanuel 5

*"Behold, the virgin shall conceive and bear a son, and they shall
call his name Immanuel" (which means, God with us).*

MATTHEW 1:23

VENI EMMANUEL
Text: Latin antiphons, 12th c.
Tr. John Mason Neale
Music: Plainsong, 13th c.

Ve - ni, ve - ni Em - man - u - el, Cap -
1. O come, O come, Em - man - u - el, and
2. O *come, Thou Rod of Jes - se, free Thine*
3. O come, Thou Day - spring from_____ on high, and
4. O *come, Thou Key of Da - vid, come and*

ti - vum sol - ve Is - ra - el, Qui ge - mit in ex -
ran - som cap - tive Is - ra - el, that mourns in lone - ly
own from Sa - tan's tyr - an - ny; from depths of hell Thy
cheer us by Thy draw - ing nigh; dis - perse the gloom - y
o - pen wide our heav'n - ly home; make safe the way that

i - li - o, Pri - va - tus De - i Fi - li - o.
ex - ile here, un - til the Son of God_____ ap - pear.
peo - ple save, and give them vic - t'ry o'er_____ the grave.
clouds_____ of night, and death's dark shad-ows put_____ to flight.
leads_____ on high, and close the path to mis - er - y.

Gau - de, gau - de! Em - man - u -
Re - joice! Re - joice! Em - man - u -

el na - sce - tur pro - te, Is - ra - el.
el shall come to thee, O Is - ra - el.

27

November 30 Come, Thou Long-Expected Jesus

TEXT: Charles Wesley ‖ b. December 18, 1707, Epworth, England
d. March 29, 1788, London, England

Charles Wesley wrote this poem five years after he wrote "Hark! the Herald Angels Sing." It was first published in 1744 in a small volume Wesley called *Hymns for the Nativity of Our Lord,* but out of a total of eighteen carols, these two are the only ones that we still sing today. But no hymn writer has more hymns known and sung today than Wesley, who is credited with 6,000 hymns. That amounts to one every day for fifty years! The eighteenth child of the son of a hymn writer and preacher, Wesley was homeschooled before attending Oxford University to receive a master's degree in classical languages and literature. In 1735, he traveled as a missionary to America with his older brother John proclaiming the gospel even before he had accepted it for himself.

TUNE: Rowland Prichard ‖ b. January 14, 1811, Graienyn, North Wales
d. January 25, 1887, Holywell, North Wales

Unfortunately, the original tune was poorly matched to this text and not often sung. But the song became loved and often sung after it was reset to the tune HYFRYDOL. Written in about 1830 by a twenty-year-old Welshman, Rowland Prichard, Hyfrydol is a Welsh name that means "cheerful"[12] and certainly fits the message of this text. The same tune is used for "Jesus, What a Friend for Sinners," which is also very "good news."

As you sing this hymn . . . it will be helpful to remember just how long expected the Messiah was for Israel. Assyria conquered Israel in 722 BC and took its people from their land. Babylon did the same to Judah in 586 BC. After that, the Jews were passed from ruler to ruler (including Alexander the Great in 536 BC), and whether in exile or back home, they experienced only a few years of independence. Eventually, the Romans took over, a rule that lasted until Jesus' birth. Imagine for a moment your nation being conquered by next-door nations, and then passed from one to another. You too would long for a Messiah, a Redeemer to set you free.

Then Jesus came. His name means savior, or "God is salvation." Did Jesus save them from a conquering country? No. He saved them from the bondage of sin and death. He is not a long-expected army general. Or a long-expected conquering ruler. Charles Spurgeon wrote, "Jesus is the name which moves the harps of heaven to melody. Jesus! The life of all our joys, the sum of all our delights, a song in a word, an ocean for comprehension, a matchless oratorio in two syllables, a gathering up of the hallelujahs of eternity in five letters."[13] So we sing, "From our fears and sins release us . . . now Thy gracious Kingdom bring."

Are you waiting for a Savior to free you from your slavery to fear and sin? There is no need to wait. He will enter your life today if you claim His forgiveness and invite Him to save you. Then you may join all Christians who wait for the appearing of our Lord Jesus Christ when He comes to earth the second time. He will "raise us to His glorious throne."

Come, Thou Long-Expected Jesus 6

And I will shake all nations, so that the treasures of all nations
shall come in, and I will fill this house with glory,
says the LORD of hosts.

HAGGAI 2:7

HYFRYDOL
Text: Charles Wesley
Music: Rowland Hugh Prichard

1. Come, Thou long - ex - pect - ed Je - sus, born to set Thy people free; from our fears and sins re - lease us; let us find our rest in Thee. Is - rael's strength and con - so - la - tion, hope of all the earth Thou art, dear De - sire of ev - 'ry na - tion, joy of ev - 'ry long - ing heart.

2. Born Thy people to de - liv - er, born a child and yet a King, born to reign in us for - ev - er, now Thy gra - cious king - dom bring. By Thine own e - ter - nal Spir - it rule in all our hearts a - lone; by Thine all - suf - fi - cient mer - it, raise us to Thy glo - rious throne.

December 1   Let All Mortal Flesh Keep Silence

TEXT: Liturgy of St. James, 5th c.   ‖   b. September 16, 1829, Rugby Rectory, England
Adapted, Gerard Moultrie   ‖   d. April 25, 1885, England

The words of this carol are a translation from a Greek Christmas Eve service of worship used in the fourth century called the Liturgy of St. James. Some scholars believe it dates back to AD 60, the same time that Paul was writing Romans. Considered to be, perhaps, the oldest liturgy developed for use in the church, it is still used today in the Eastern Orthodox Church. In 1864, Gerard Moultrie translated this text into English. An Oxford graduate who held many positions as both educator and clergy, he is credited with translating dozens of Greek, Latin, and German hymn texts. The word "liturgy" means the public work of the congregation and refers to the words they use in worship, often repeated each week. With these words, the congregation expresses profound awe and wonder at the incarnation of Jesus. It is a majestic picture of the nativity and the whole story of salvation, quite different from the narrative or folksy description found in many carols. The text was used in preparation for the celebration of the Eucharist or Communion, with reference to Jesus offering a "gift of Himself as heavenly food."

TUNE: Traditional French Melody, 17th c.   ‖
Arranged, Ralph Vaughan Williams

PICARDY is a medieval folk melody and thought to be named after the province in France where it was first used. Ralph Vaughan Williams arranged it for this text in 1906. It has a chantlike style in a modal or minor key similar to the sound from ancient worship you might hear in cathedrals. Notice that the text was written 1200 years earlier.

As you sing this hymn . . . think on why Habakkuk 2:20 would instruct, "Let all the earth keep silence before him." Fallen human beings are not typically slow to speak their minds. Even if our lips are silent, our hearts burst forth with excuses and arguments and justifications and demands. But now Habakkuk says to stay silent. Why?

The author of Ecclesiastes requires a similar silence before God and gives an explanation: "Guard your steps when you go to the house of God. To draw near to listen is better than to offer the sacrifice of fools . . . Be not rash with your mouth, nor let your heart be hasty to utter a word before God, for God is in heaven and you are on earth" (Eccl. 5:1–2). Do you see the "for" in the last phrase? It alerts us to the explanation: God is in heaven; you are on earth.

God is the Creator; you are the creature. God is awesome and majestic and worthy of all praise; you were created to give praise. Who are we to talk back to Him?

Now consider the first line: "Let all mortal flesh keep silence, and with fear and trembling stand; ponder nothing earthly minded, for with blessing in his hand, Christ our God to earth descendeth, our full homage to demand." The mighty and awesome One, who dwells in unapproachable light, whose throne room no soul has seen and returned to tell of it, came from heaven to earth and was born in a manger.

The time will come for singing, but shouldn't the first response be a stop-in-our-tracks, drop-our-weapons, look-up-from-our-work, even-the-wind-and-waves-halt kind of silence?

Let All Mortal Flesh Keep Silence

7

But the LORD is in his holy temple;
let all the earth keep silence before him.

HABAKKUK 2:20

PICARDY
Text: Liturgy of St. James, 5th c.
Adapt. Gerard Moultrie
Music: Traditional French melody 17th c.

1. Let all mor-tal flesh keep__ si - lence, and with fear and
2. King of kings, yet born of__ Ma - ry, as of old on
3. Rank on rank the host of__ heav - en spreads its van-guard
4. At His feet the six - winged ser - aph; cher - u - bim, with

trem - bling__ stand; pon-der noth-ing earth - ly__ mind - ed,
earth He__ stood, Lord of lords, in hu - man__ ves - ture,
on the__ way, as the Light of light de - scend - eth
sleep - less__ eye, veil their fac - es to the__ Pres - ence,

for with bless - ing in His__ hand, Christ our God to earth de -
in the bod - y and the__ blood, He will give to all the
from the realms of end - less__ day, that the pow'rs of hell may
as with cease -less voice they__ cry, "Al - le - lu - ia, al - le -

scend - eth, our full hom-age to de - mand.
faith - ful His own self for heav'n - ly__ food.
van - ish as the dark-ness clears a - way.
lu - ia, al - le - lu - ia, Lord Most__ High!"

31

December 2　Of the Father's Love Begotten

TEXT: Aurelius Clemens Prudentius ‖ b. 348, Spain
Translated, John Mason Neale, 1854 ‖ d. 413, Spain
and Henry W. Baker, 1859

This is the oldest hymn text in our collection of carols and quite possibly in all hymnals. It is originally from an ancient Latin poem, *Corde natus,* by the poet Aurelius Clemens Prudentius, who was born into an upper-class Christian family in a Roman province in northern Spain and became a lawyer, twice serving as the governor of his province. He even received a high office in the court of the Christian Emperor Theodosius. Prudentius was loyal to the Roman Empire and considered it to be an "instrument in the hands of Providence for the advancement of Christianity."[14] At the age of fifty-seven, he decided that his public work was of little value and retired to write religious poetry. Many of his poems became hymns and were important to Christians in the Middle Ages.

The version we sing was first translated into English by John Mason Neale. Neale helped translate over 400 hymns and is well-known for his English carol "Good King Wenceslas." Henry Baker later edited and extended it to the present version. Baker, an English clergyman, served as the editor-in-chief of the Anglican *Hymns Ancient and Modern,* a historic hymnal that sold sixty million copies. The original poem had nine stanzas including one to encourage all generations to sing. "Thee let old men, thee let young men, Thee let boys in chorus sing; Matrons, virgins, little maidens, With glad voices answering: Let their guileless songs re-echo, And the heart its music bring, evermore and evermore!"

TUNE: 12th Century Plainsong ‖

This may also be the oldest tune in our hymnal. For centuries, the music in the Catholic and Eastern Orthodox churches consisted of plainsong or chant. Plainsong is monophonic (mono: "one"; phonic: "sound"), which means there is a single, unaccompanied melodic line. It has a freer rhythm, unlike the metered rhythm of Western music as we know it. Plainsong DIVINUM MYSTERIUM, a divine mystery, was paired with this poem and first appeared in a Finnish songbook in 1582.

As you sing this hymn . . . this chantlike melody offers a sense of wonder and awe. Its rise and fall pull back the curtain, revealing a truth beyond reason or logic. The tune is well-named as a divine mystery. The apostle Paul uses the word mystery twenty-one times throughout his writings. For instance, he observes, "Beyond all question, the mystery from which true godliness springs is great" (1 Tim. 3:16 NIV). What is the mystery? It's the good news formerly concealed but now revealed in Jesus Christ. Paul continues, "He appeared in the flesh, was vindicated by the Spirit, was seen by angels, was preached among the nations, was believed on in the world, was taken up in glory." It is no wonder, then, that the hymn's text points to the superlatives of God's nature. He is the Alpha and Omega, the source and the ending of all things.

Concerning this mystery, the hymn writer declares, "Let no tongue on earth be silent." From "evermore to evermore" we will grow in our understanding and wonder. But while on this earth we will never, nor do we need to, fully understand the mystery. Only to accept it with gratitude!

Of the Father's Love Begotten

8

*In the beginning was the Word. . . . And the Word
became flesh . . . and we have seen his glory,
glory as of the only Son from the Father.*

JOHN 1:1, 14

DIVINUM MYSTERIUM
Text: Aurelius Clemens Prudentius
Music: Plainsong, 12th c.

1. Of the Fa-ther's love be - got - ten   ere the worlds be - gan___ to be,
2. O that birth for - ev - er   bless - ed,   when the Vir - gin, full___ of grace,
3. O ye heights of heav'n a - dore_ Him,   an - gel hosts, His prais - es sing;
4. Christ, to Thee with God the Fa - ther,   and, O Ho - ly   Ghost, to Thee,

He   is Al - pha and O - me - ga,   He the Source, the End - ing He,
by   the Ho - ly Ghost con - ceiv - ing,   bore the Sav - ior of___ our race;
powers, do-min-ions, bow be - fore_ Him,   and ex - tol our God_ and King;
hymn and chant and high thanks-giv - ing,   and un - wea - ried prais - es be:

of   the things that are, that have_____ been,
and   the Babe, the world's Re - deem - - - er,
let   no tongue on earth be si - - - lent,
hon - or, glo - ry, and do - min - - - ion,

and that fu - ture years shall see,   ev - er -more and ev - er - more!__
first re -vealed His sa - cred face,   ev - er -more and ev - er - more!__
ev - ery voice in con -cert ring,   ev - er -more and ev - er - more!__
and e - ter - nal vic - to - ry,   ev - er -more and ev - er - more!__

TEXT: Philip Doddridge ‖ b. June 26, 1702, London, England
d. October 26, 1751, Lisbon, Portugal

Philip Doddridge was the last and twentieth child born to Daniel Doddridge, a London dealer in oil and pickles! His grandfather had been a nonconformist minister and was ejected from the Church of England for his radical positions. Before he could read, Doddridge's mother, Elizabeth, taught him the Bible from their home's blue Dutch wall tiles embedded with Scriptures. Sadly, both parents died by the time he was twelve, and by age thirteen, his guardian had squandered Doddridge's inheritance. However, Presbyterian minister Samuel Clark cared for him as a son, overseeing Doddridge's education and encouraging him to become a minister. At Clark's funeral, Doddridge preached, "To him, under God . . . I owe even myself, and all my opportunities of public usefulness in the church."[15]

Doddridge followed the path of nonconforming ministers, and in 1723, became pastor of an independent church in Northampton. His book *The Rise and Progress of Religion in the Soul* was referred to by Charles Spurgeon as "that holy book." It also influenced William Wilberforce, the anti-slave trade campaigner, to become a Christian. Along with a New Testament commentary and numerous theological works, Doddridge wrote over 400 hymns. His hymn "O Happy Day" is known today because of a joyous Black-gospel setting in 1967 by the Edwin Hawkins singers. Despite a dismal early childhood, Doddridge found great joy in his salvation and walk with God.

TUNE: Attributed to Thomas Haweis ‖ b. January 1, 1732, Cornwall, England
d. February 11, 1820, Bath, England

Though raised in poverty, Thomas Haweis (pronounced, "hawes") was educated at Oxford and became an apothecary and physician. After being introduced to the gospel, he left this career for ministry. He created a book of 139 of his hymns called *Carmina Christi* or *Hymns to the Savior*. CHESTERFIELD (also known as RICHMOND) is one of the best marriages of tune and text. The first four notes use the same interval motif as the trumpet "Call to Post" in horse racing! The melody winds in a rising succession to a climax on the words "throne," "burst," "grace," and "ring" for each stanza.

As you sing this hymn . . . a smile will come to your face as you sing, "Hark! the glad sound!" Imagine Jesus' arrival in a royal caravan preceded by heralding trumpets. With joy, we anticipate what the arrival means—the release of captives, the opening of prisons, the healing of broken hearts, and the riches of grace for the humble poor. Consider the prophecy in Isaiah 61:1 and Jesus' own declaration in Luke 4:18 from which Doddridge draws, "The Spirit of the Lord is upon me, because he has anointed me to proclaim good news to the poor. He has sent me to proclaim liberty to the captives and recovering of sight to the blind, to set at liberty those who are oppressed."

Of course, Christ's coming to Bethlehem had none of the hymn's fanfare apart from an amazing angel choir! Today gladness is exclaimed in "Hosannas" (st. 4) for this coming Prince of Peace. Even the arches of heaven, Doddridge proclaims, are ringing with praise of His name. Make this hymn your proclamation of true Advent joy!

Hark the Glad Sound! The Savior Comes 9

Fear not, for behold, I bring you good news
of great joy that will be for all the people.

LUKE 2:10

CHESTERFIELD
Text: Philip Doddridge
Music: Thomas Haweis

1. Hark the glad sound! The Sav - ior comes, the Sav - ior
2. He comes the cap - tives to__ re - lease, in Sa - tan's
3. He comes the bro - ken heart_ to bind, the bleed - ing
4. Our glad ho - san - nas, Prince_ of Peace, Your wel - come

prom - ised long;_____ Let ev - 'ry heart_ pre -
pri - son held._____ The gates_ of brass_ be -
soul_ to cure,_____ and with_ the trea - sures
shall_ pro - claim,_____ and heav'n's e - ter - nal

pare_ a throne, and ev - 'ry voice_ a song.
fore_ Him burst; the i - ron fet - ters yield.
of__ His grace to en - rich_ the hum - ble poor.
arch - es ring with Your_ be - lov - ed name.

The NATIVITY

THE WORD "NATIVITY" is derived from the Latin *nativus*, which means "arisen by birth." Although technically we could use the word to describe any birth, it has become synonymous with the birth of Jesus. Nativities created as art, models, carvings, or even live demonstrations are common Christmas decorations depicting the night of Jesus' birth.

Although Christmas Day is celebrated in only twenty-four hours, the immensity of its meaning and significance demands much more time and consideration. We do not know the exact day or even the year of Jesus' birth, and few believe it was December 25 or even in the winter. The shepherds would unlikely have been out in their fields by night! So this creates a problem with some Christmas carols that speak of snow and cold. Even though our calendar implies that year one is the first year of Christ's life, most scholars believe the year was somewhere between 6 and 4 BC. Yet the most important issue is not the precise date of when it happened, but that it happened on a precise date. In his book *The Truth of God Incarnate*, Michael Green defines the incarnation as being "the way and time that God made Himself known specifically and personally by taking our human nature into Himself, by coming amongst us as a particular man, without in any way ceasing to be the eternal and infinite God."[16]

Many people struggle with understanding or believing in the mystery of the incarnation. Few doctrines are as attacked as this one, and one can sympathize with the challenges. There is nothing in the history of our world that equals the power and mystery of God becoming man, especially to be born in a manger. It is a radical claim. Yet the Bible says it is true, and the doctrine is central to the entire Christian story. If God had not become man, He could not have borne the sin of humankind as a representative man. And if God did not become man, He could not have lived as the perfect human, redeeming once more what it means to be human. In short, if God did not become man, we could not be saved. You must believe in His deity *and* His humanity, or else you believe in a false Jesus.

In his book *God in the Dock*, C. S. Lewis observes,

> The Christian story is precisely the story of one grand miracle, the Christian assertion being that what is beyond all space and time, what is uncreated, eternal, come into nature, into human nature, descended into His own universe, and rose again, bringing nature up with Him. It is precisely one great miracle. If you take that away there is nothing specifically Christian left.[17]

God revealed Himself in Jesus. So Jesus said, "Anyone who has seen me has seen the Father" (John 14:9 NIV). To deny the incarnation removes the hope for humanity that the Creator God has such love for His creation that He would become one of us. If one can believe in the incarnation, it is possible to believe in the death and resurrection of Jesus. How ironic that the wood of a tender manger or cradle was made of the same substance as the cruel cross. The cradle led to the cross, which reveals the extent to which God would go to save us from our sins.

As you meditate on and sing these hymns of the nativity, notice how many tie the cradle and the cross together. Allow the songs of Christmas to take you far beyond the manger. As far as we know, only Mary was present at both the cradle and the cross. But by the inspiration and revelation of Scripture so often quoted in these hymns, you can see them both. May the incarnation change your life forever.

IT WAS THE WINTER WILD,
While the heaven-born child
All meanly wrapt in the rude manger lies;
Nature in awe to him
Had doffed her gaudy trim,
With her great master so to sympathize:
It was no season then for her
To wanton with the Sun her lusty paramour.

.   .   .   .   .   .

No war, or battle's sound
Was heard the world around:
The idle spear and shield were high uphung;
The hooked chariot stood
Unstained with hostile blood,
The trumpet spake not to the armed throng,
And kings sat still with awful eye,
As if they surely knew their sovereign Lord was by.

But peaceful was the night,
Wherein the prince of light
His reign of peace upon the earth began:
The winds, with wonder whist,
Smoothly the waters kissed,
Whispering new joys to the mild ocean,
Who now hath quite forgot to rave,
While birds of calm sit brooding on the charmed wave.

The stars with deep amaze,
Stand fixed in steadfast gaze,
Bending one way their precious influence,
And will not take their flight,
For all the morning light,
Or Lucifer that often warned them thence;
But in their glimmering orbs did glow,
Until their Lord Himself bespake, and bid them go.

And though the shady gloom
Had given day her room,
The sun himself withheld his wonted speed,
And hid his head for shame,
As his inferior flame,
The new-enlightened world no more should need;
He saw a greater sun appear
Than his bright throne or burning axletree could bear.

The shepherds on the lawn
Or ere the point of dawn,
Sat simply chatting in a rustic row;
Full little thought they then,
That the mighty Pan
Was kindly come to live with them below;
Perhaps their loves, or else their sheep,
Was all that did their silly thoughts so busy keep.

When such music sweet
Their hearts and ears did greet,
As never was by mortal finger struck,
Divinely-warbled voice
Answering the stringed noise,
As all their souls in blissful rapture took:
The air such pleasure loath to lose,
With thousand echoes still prolongs each heavenly close.

.   .   .   .   .   .

At last surrounds their sight
A globe of circular light,
That with long beams the shamefaced night arrayed,
The helmed cherubim,
And sworded seraphim,
Are seen in glittering ranks with wings displayed,
Harping in loud and solemn choir,
With unexpressive notes to heaven's new-born heir.

JOHN MILTON, 1608–1674[18]

December 4   Angels from the Realms of Glory

TEXT: James Montgomery ‖ b. November 4, 1771, Irvine, Ayrshire, Scotland
d. April 30, 1854, Sheffield, England

When James Montgomery was five years old, his parents, Moravian missionaries, felt called to the West Indies, and he was sent to a Moravian community in Ireland. Five years later, both parents died on the mission field. As a result, his formative years were tough, and he even became homeless. Montgomery loved to write and was skilled at poetry. He wrote odes on everything from loneliness to faith. As a young man, he founded a newspaper and used it in rebellion against the English rule over Ireland. Twice he landed in prison because of his fiery editorials.

Through it all, Montgomery was drawn to the Bible where he searched for understanding of his parents' faith. On Christmas Eve, 1816, he presented a poem titled "Nativity." The poem came as a surprise to many. Rather than a message of anger and divisiveness, it spoke of unity, even between Irish and English, under a common allegiance to the babe of Bethlehem. The poem eventually was renamed "Angels from the Realms of Glory." A long-ago deleted stanza reveals James's search for meaning: "Sinners, wrung with true repentance, / Doom'd for guilt to endless pains, / Justice now revokes the sentence, / Mercy calls you—break your chains."[19]

TUNE: Henry T. Smart ‖ b. October 26, 1813, London, England
d. July 6, 1879, London, England

Henry Smart was the son of a music publisher and became one of England's most skilled organists and composers. Traditionally, church music was primarily composed of monophonic or polyphonic chants (no harmony) and performed by trained musicians so that the congregation became spectators. As one who rebelled against this, Smart published new songbooks with harmonized melodies and singable melodies. Sadly, by the age of eighteen, he was already losing his sight. Blind by 1836, twenty years after Montgomery wrote the poem, Smart wrote this memorable tune. In God's providence, "Angels from the Realms of Glory" was sung in Anglican churches throughout London, the very city where Montgomery had, years before, also led a rebellion over congregational singing and music styles. REGENT SQUARE takes the name of Regent Square Presbyterian Church in London. Many call this hymn the best-written Christmas carol of all time.

As you sing this hymn . . . you are reminded of the angels, the shepherds, the wise men (sages) and possibly Anna and Simeon who "watched with hope and fear." What did they have in common? Worship. Every character in the Christmas story shares the same response: bowing down in humble adoration. They are models for us to be "before the altar bending." The final stanza ends with the assurance from Philippians 2 that someday every knee will bow and every tongue confess that Jesus is Lord. Meditate now on Paul's profound declaration of future universal worship, #39 in "Christmas in the Bible."

The repeated refrain is a call to worship within a rising melody that culminates in the strongest declaration that this newborn baby is the King! Like a sermon that teaches the history and proclaims the truth, it asks—what are you going to do about it? Will you worship too? Come and worship!

Angels from the Realms of Glory

That at the name of Jesus, every knee should bow,
in heaven and on earth and under the earth,
and every tongue confess that Jesus Christ is Lord,
to the glory of God the Father.

PHILIPPIANS 2:10–11

REGENT SQUARE
Text: James Montgomery
Music: Henry T. Smart

1. An - gels from the realms of glo - ry, wing your flight o'er all the earth;
2. Shep-herds, in the fields a - bid - ing, watch-ing o'er your flocks by night,
3. Sag - es, leave your con - tem-pla-tions, bright-er vi-sions beam a - far;
4. Saints be-fore the al - tar bend-ing, watch-ing long in hope and fear,
5. Though an in - fant now we view Him He will share His Fa-ther's throne,

ye who sang cre - a - tion's sto - ry, now pro-claim Mes - si - ah's birth:
God with us is now re - sid - ing, yon-der shines the_ in - fant Light:
seek the great De - sire of Na - tions, ye have seen His_ na - tal star:
sud-den - ly the Lord, de-scend-ing, in His tem - ple_ shall ap - pear.
gath - er all the na - tions to Him; ev - ery knee shall then bow down.

Come and wor- ship, come and wor- ship, wor - ship Christ, the new-born King.

December 5 Angels We Have Heard on High

TEXT: Traditional French Carol ‖

No one knows who wrote the words to this carol. Although first sung in nineteenth-century France, the chorus is in Latin, suggesting the carol was written much earlier. Hymnologists agree that the author had an excellent knowledge of Scripture, as well as the skill to shape biblical text into verse. Some believe it might have been written by a monk in the early Roman Catholic Church. The text first appeared in print in French in 1855, but is known to have been sung at least fifty years earlier. It was translated into English by a priest named James Chadwick. *Excelsis* (pronounced eck-SHELL-sees) means "highest." *Deo* (pronounced DEH-aw) means "God." *Gloria in Excelsis Deo* means "glory to God in the highest."

TUNE: Traditional French Melody ‖ b. September 14, 1887, Seabright, New Jersey
Arranged, Edward S. Barnes ‖ d. February 14, 1958, Idyllwild, California

Although GLORIA is a traditional French melody, the modern arrangement we sing was adapted in 1937 by American Edward S. Barnes. Educated at Yale University, he studied with the great composer and organist, Louis Verne, in Paris. Barnes was organist at two churches in New York City, an Episcopal Church in Philadelphia, and finally the First Presbyterian Church in Santa Monica. He composed organ symphonies and organ arrangements of sacred music. The cascading melody in the refrain imitates the growing host of angels over the shepherds' field.

As you sing this hymn . . . imagine the shepherds trying to retell their experience of seeing a multitude of angels appear over their Bethlehem field one dark night. Words would be wholly inadequate! Imagine the sound of angels singing! Perhaps one group sang, "Glory to God in the highest," another group, "Peace on earth," and a third group, "Goodwill to men!" How would you respond if even one angel suddenly appeared to tell you about Jesus' birth?

And why did God choose lowly shepherds as the audience for the greatest pronouncement, with the greatest song, by the greatest choir ever heard? Why were shepherds the first to see the baby Jesus? Was it because Jesus would be called the Lamb of God or that He is the Great Shepherd? Many people God called to serve Him were shepherds, including Moses and David. Yet, they were the lowest people in society. David declared: "We are his people and the sheep of his pasture" (Ps. 100:3). God sent angels to welcome shepherds—as He welcomes you—to the manger.

Because the refrain of *"Gloria in Excelsis Deo"* is so wonderfully familiar, a countermelody is offered for lower voices. If you are singing with a group, learn the countermelody alone as its own melody, then combine the two like a growing host of angels praising God in the highest.

Angels We Have Heard on High

11

*Glory to God in the highest, and on earth peace
among those with whom he is pleased!*

LUKE 2:14

GLORIA

Text: Traditional French carol
Music: Traditional French melody, Arr. Edward S. Barnes

1. An - gels we have heard on high, sweet - ly sing-ing o'er the plains,
2. Shep-herds, why this ju - bi - lee? Why your joy - ous strains pro-long?
3. Come to Beth - le - hem and see Him whose birth the an - gels sing;

and the moun-tains in re-ply ech - o back their joy - ous strains.
Say what may the tid - ings be, which in-spire your heav'n - ly song?
come, a - dore on bend - ed knee Christ the Lord, the new - born King.

Glo - - - - - - ri - a

in ex - cel - sis De - o, Glo - - -

- - - ri - a in ex - cel - sis De - - o.

TEXT: Charles Wesley   b. December 18, 1707, Epworth, England
d. March 29, 1788, London

The first line of Charles Wesley's poem reads, "Hark! How all the welkin rings, glory to the King of kings." *Welkin* is an Old English word that means, "the vault of the sky" or "heaven."[20] It exclaims that all of heaven rings glory! A friend of the Wesleys, the famous reformed evangelist George Whitefield, took the liberty of publishing Wesley's carol, changing the words to proclaim who sings glory. "Hark! the herald angels sing, glory to the newborn King." Wesley was furious with his friend! He did not mind others copying his poetry, but he did not like them changing the words. Although Wesley himself never would sing the changed words, these are the ones that gained popularity the world over.

TUNE: Felix Mendelssohn   b. February 3, 1809, Hamburg, Germany
d. November 4, 1847, Leipzig, Germany

Mendelssohn, a famous composer of the nineteenth century, was born into a wealthy Jewish family in Berlin, Germany, and later converted to Christianity. Some of his best-known works include *A Midsummer Night's Dream* and *Elijah*. A significant contribution he made to Western culture was the revival of the music of Johann Sebastian Bach, which was mostly unknown a hundred years after that composer's death. In 1840, Mendelssohn wrote this tune as a tribute to Johann Gutenberg, the inventor of the printing press. He expected that although its melody would be loved by singers, it would never do for sacred words; however, one of his singers, William H. Cummings, found that the tune perfectly fit Wesley's words. Neither the hymn writer, Wesley, nor the composer, Mendelssohn, ever knew their creative works were combined into this beloved carol. The tune's name is MENDELSSOHN.

As you sing this hymn . . . you are a "herald," announcing the most important event in history: the very God of heaven has come to earth to save us! You may picture long, gleaming herald trumpets used in fanfares. The fanfare here is the refrain, "Hark! [Listen attentively!] The herald angels sing, 'Glory to the newborn King!'" As you sing, you become a preacher of the good news of the gospel.

This popular Christmas carol is often sung by both believing and nonbelieving soloists and choirs. Unfortunately, few stop to think of the significance and power in such phrases as "veiled in flesh the Godhead see," "incarnate Deity," "born to give them second birth," or "God and sinners reconciled." It is easy to travel on the friendly path of a familiar melody and fail to concentrate on the words.

As is characteristic of the hymns of Charles Wesley, every phrase is packed with theology and allusions to or quotations of Scripture. The following list of verses are found in this carol: Luke 2:10–14; 2 Corinthians 5:19; Revelation 15:4; Hebrews 1:6; Matthew 1:21–23; John 1:1; Philippians 2:7; Isaiah 9:6; Malachi 4:2; and 1 Peter 1:3. Reading each one before you sing will give you a deeper appreciation of songs written from Scripture rather than simply from personal experience or emotions. This song is saturated with the gospel message, and you will gain an overview of how that message is found throughout the Bible.

Hark! the Herald Angels Sing

12

*Suddenly there was with the angel a multitude
of the heavenly host praising God and saying,
"Glory to God in the highest . . . !"*

LUKE 2:13–14

MENDELSSOHN
Text: Charles Wesley
Music: Felix Mendelssohn

1. Hark! the her - ald an - gels sing,__ "Glo - ry to the new-born King;
2. Christ, by high - est heav'n a - dored, Christ, the ev - er - last - ing Lord!
3. Hail the heav'n-born Prince of Peace! Hail the Sun of Righ-teous-ness!

peace on earth, and mer - cy mild,_ God and sin - ners rec - on - ciled!"
Late in time be - hold Him come,_ off-spring of the Vir - gin's womb.
Light and life to all He brings, ris'n with heal - ing in His wings.

Joy - ful, all ye na - tions, rise,__ join the tri - umph of the skies;_
Veiled in flesh the God-head see;__ hail th'in - car - nate De - i - ty,__
Mild He lays His glo - ry by,__ born that man no more may die,__

with th'an-gel - ic host pro-claim, "Christ is__ born in Beth - le - hem!"
pleased as man with men to dwell, Je - sus,__ our Em - man - u - el.
born to raise the sons of earth, born to__ give them sec - ond birth.

Hark! the her - ald an - gels sing, "Glo - ry__ to the new-born King!"

45

TEXT: Jaroslav J. Vajda ‖ b. April 28, 1919, Lorain, Ohio
d. May 10, 2008, Webster Groves, Missouri

Jaroslav Vajda was a frail child who had chronic bronchitis. Yet by the age of twelve, he was playing the violin in the Chicago Youth Symphony. At the age of eighteen, Vajda translated classical Slovak poetry into English. He became a Lutheran pastor and the author of 225 hymns, although he did not write his first hymn until age forty-nine. Today his hymns are found in almost fifty hymnals. A friend and Lutheran educator said of Vajda's texts: "One is always struck by the strong theological thrust of Jary's texts—biblically grounded, theologically informed, and rooted in Trinitarian theology."[21]

At his death, Vajda was lauded as "the dean of hymn writers in North America" and "the poet laureate of the hymn world." He claimed he learned to write hymns by translating poetry. He humbly stated, "My hymns are what they are: poetic expressions of thanks to God. They are my grateful reaction—my praise and wonder and exclamation—to the love and glory of God."[22]

TUNE: Carl F. Schalk ‖ b. 1929, Chicago, Illinois

Carl Schalk is a noted composer, author, and lecturer and a professor of music emeritus at Concordia University, River Forest, Illinois, where he taught from 1965 until his retirement in 1994. Schalk was a member of the Inter-Lutheran Commission on Worship, which produced the *Lutheran Book of Worship* in 1978. He is a fellow of the Hymn Society of the United States and Canada and was made an honorary life member of the Association of Lutheran Church Musicians. His numerous choral compositions are published by a wide array of publishers, and he has written over eighty hymn tunes and carols. This tune was originally written as a choral work but is now sung as a hymn and loved worldwide by Lutheran worshipers.

As you sing this hymn . . . you are walking in the shepherds' sandals. You have heard the angels' announcement and come in this modern day to see for yourself. Perhaps initially you came with "half-belief" and "pounding heart," only grateful for the opportunity to join them. But today, we come to the manger with hindsight, for we know that baby did cry for us. You too remember the prophecies of Isaiah and the anticipation of a Messiah. But today you understand that this has been fulfilled, and this child is the Son of God and the Prince of Peace who wants to enter your life.

The final stanza describes Jesus burning His way into our heart, "unasked, unforced, unearned." What a great deal of theology is implied in just three words. Meditate for a few minutes on this wonder that the King of the Universe comes to you in such a powerful but gentle way.

The story of the shepherds is an analogy of our lives. They heard the message from the angels, and they believed it. So they went to Jesus, and then went out and told everyone. Similarly, God reveals Himself to us through a sermon, or someone sharing, or reading His Word. We hear it, we believe it, and we act on it, telling others what we have learned—just as the shepherds did.

Where Shepherds Lately Knelt

13

*"Let us go over to Bethlehem and see this thing that
has happened, which the Lord has made known to us."
And they went with haste.*

LUKE 2:15–16

MANGER SONG
Text: Jaroslav J. Vajda
Music: Carl F. Schalk

1. Where shep-herds late-ly knelt and kept the an-gel's word,
2. In that un-like-ly place I find Him as they said:
3. How should I not have known I - sa - iah would be there,
4. Can I, will I for - get how Love was born, and burned

I come in half-be-lief, a pil-grim strange-ly stirred,
sweet new-born babe, how frail! and in a man-ger bed,
his proph-e - cies ful-filled? With pound-ing heart I stare:
its way in - to my heart—un - asked, un - forced, un -earned,

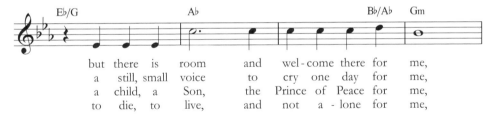

but there is room and wel-come there for me,
a still, small voice to cry one day for me,
a child, a Son, the Prince of Peace for me,
to die, to live, and not a - lone for me,

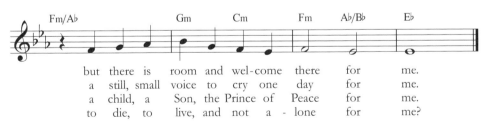

but there is room and wel-come there for me.
a still, small voice to cry one day for me.
a child, a Son, the Prince of Peace for me.
to die, to live, and not a - lone for me?

TEXT: Edmond H. Sears ‖ b. April 6, 1810, Sandisfield, Massachusetts
d. January 14, 1876, Weston, Massachusetts

Born and raised on a farm, Edmond Sears excelled in school and loved poetry. He wrote, "when at work, some poem was always singing through my brain."[23] At Union College, Schenectady, New York, he won prizes in poetry. He graduated from Harvard Divinity School and pastored three Unitarian churches. Sears was known by Unitarians as a conservative. In his 1875 book, *Sermons and Songs of the Christian Life*, he wrote, "Although I was educated in the Unitarian denomination, I believe and preach the Divinity of Christ."[24] In 1849, at the request of a minister friend, Sears wrote the poem "It Came upon the Midnight Clear" for a Sunday school Christmas celebration. The original includes a third stanza missing from hymnals and reflects the great pain of the Civil War and Sears's staunch position against slavery: "But with the woes of sin and strife the world has suffered long: beneath the angel-strain have rolled two thousand years of wrong: And man, at war with man, heard not the love-song which they bring:
O hush the noise, ye men of strife, and hear the angels sing!"

TUNE: Richard S. Willis ‖ b. February 10, 1819, Boston, Massachusetts
d. May 7, 1900, Detroit, Michigan

Various tunes are used for this text, but CAROL is familiar to Americans. Willis was a graduate of Yale University and did further music studies in Germany where he became friends with Felix Mendelssohn. This tune was printed with Sears's poem in the Methodist hymnal of 1878.

As you sing this hymn . . . notice the carol never mentions the birth of Christ, but only the angels' announcement. Some speculate that despite his claims, Sears didn't believe in the deity of Christ. However, he calls Him "heaven's King." Certainly, the focus concerns the words "Peace on earth, goodwill to men." Soldiers in WWI and WWII loved this carol for its relevant language of "crushing loads," "sad and lowly plains," and "babel sounds." In our world, these things still are present today. Why? Was the angels' declaration simply a nice Christmas card slogan that would never come to pass?

Unfortunately, Sears did not have an accurate translation of Luke 2:14, which reads, "Glory to God in the highest, and on earth peace among those with whom he is pleased!" Consider for a moment: With whom is God pleased? Hebrews 11:6 says that "without faith it is impossible to please God" (NIV). In our world there will never be universal, lasting peace. We should seek it and pray for it but understand that true and complete peace only comes to those who by faith accept the reason for His birth.

Poetic license may have fostered the extrabiblical descriptions Sears used, such as the angels appearing at midnight or their hovering wings and harps of gold. But the carol reminds us that many in our world are still in great pain and under crushing loads of sorrow. Pray as you sing that salvation from the Prince of Peace may bring inner peace to hearts that are open to make Him their King.

It Came upon the Midnight Clear 14

*"I bring you good news of great joy that will be for
all the people. . . ." And suddenly there was with the angel
a multitude of the heavenly host praising God.*

LUKE 2:10 & 13

Praise him, all his angels; praise him, all his hosts!

PSALM 148:2

CAROL
Text: Edmond H. Sears
Music: Richard S. Willis

1. It came up - on___ the mid - night clear, that glo - rious song___ of old,_____ from an - gels bend - ing near the earth to touch their harps___ of gold:_____ "Peace on the earth,___ good will to men, from heav'ns all - gra - cious King."_____ The world in sol - emn still - ness lay to hear the an - gels sing.___

2. Still through the clo - ven skies they come, with peace - ful wings un - furled,_____ and still their heav'n - ly mu - sic floats o'er all the wea - ry world;_____ a - bove its sad___ and low - ly plains they bend___ on hov - 'ring wing:_____ and ev - er o'er___ its Ba - bel sounds the bless - ed an - gels sing.___

3. And ye, be - neath___ life's crush - ing load, whose forms are bend - ing low,_____ who toil a - long___ the climb - ing way with pain - ful steps___ and slow,_____ look now! for glad___ and gold - en hours come swift - ly on___ the wing:_____ O rest be - side___ the wea - ry road and hear the an - gels sing.___

4. For lo, the days___ are has - t'ning on, by proph - et seen___ of - old,_____ when with the ev - er - cir - cling years shall come the time___ fore - told,_____ when peace shall o - ver all the earth its an - cient splen - dors fling,_____ and all the world give back the song which now the an - gels sing.___

December 9   O Little Town of Bethlehem

TEXT: Phillips Brooks   ‖   b. December 13, 1835, Boston, Massachusetts
d. January 23, 1893, Boston, Massachusetts

Phillips Brooks, called by some "the greatest preacher of the 19th century," was born in Massachusetts and attended the Boston Latin School, then Harvard University. The Phillips Brooks House at Harvard is named for him. He attended the Episcopal Theological Seminary in Virginia and became a priest in 1860, just before the Civil War. He is remembered for his support ending slavery, and he gave the funeral message for Abraham Lincoln.

Brooks wrote the carol for the children in his Sunday school when he was rector of Holy Trinity Church in Philadelphia. It was inspired by a trip he had taken to the Holy Land (Israel) in 1865. Wanting to get away from the other travelers there for the holidays, he borrowed a horse and rode from Jerusalem to Bethlehem to assist with the Christmas Eve service. He describes it:

> I remember standing in the old church in Bethlehem, close to the spot where Jesus was born, when the whole church was ringing hour after hour with splendid hymns of praise to God, how again and again it seemed as if I could hear voices I knew well, telling each other of the Wonderful Night of the Saviour's birth.[25]

TUNE: Lewis H. Redner   ‖   b. December 15, 1830, Philadelphia, Pennsylvania
d. August 29, 1908, Atlantic City, New Jersey

Brooks asked the organist at his church to write a tune for his hymn text. The story goes that Lewis Redner, who was also the Sunday school superintendent, was having difficulty writing it, until it finally came to him on Christmas Eve. It was first performed on December 27, 1868. The tune, ST. LOUIS, is possibly Brooks's play on words with Redner's first name.

As you sing this hymn . . . you are singing of the hometown of Ruth and of King David, where the prophet Micah precisely prophecied as Jesus' birthplace over 700 years earlier. (See "Christmas in the Bible," #8). An oft-overlooked wonder is that God ordained a worldwide census by the emperor of Rome so that the two people He had foreordained as Jesus' parents had to travel from Nazareth to Bethlehem. Lineage was an important part of God's design for the family of His Son, and Scripture lists Joseph's family tree in both Matthew and Luke. Jesus came from the royal line of King David.

Imagine you are one of the children in Brooks's Sunday school class 150 years ago. What an ideal picture he paints of shining light coming to the dark streets. What a sound of silence he describes when such a momentous event is taking place. Can you picture yourself there?

Though still a tourist location, today Bethlehem is not so inviting, as the Arab, Jewish, and Christian conflicts have made it a somewhat dangerous place to visit. What is the answer for Bethlehem and for all without peace? "Where meek souls will receive Him still," speaking of those who can admit they need help, "the dear Christ enters in." And when He enters, He imparts the blessings of heaven, forgiveness from sin, and His continual, sustaining presence for troubled people in a troubled world. The last sentence is an earnest prayer we pray: "Abide with us, our Lord Emmanuel."

O Little Town of Bethlehem

15

But you, Bethlehem Ephrathah, though you are small...
out of you will come for me one
who will be ruler over Israel.

MICAH 5:2 NIV

ST. LOUIS
Text: Phillips Brooks
Music: Lewis H. Redner

1. O lit-tle town of Beth-le-hem, how still we__ see thee lie;
2. For Christ is born of Mar-y and gath-ered__ all a-bove,
3. How si-lent-ly, how si-lent-ly, the won-drous gift is giv'n!
4. O Ho-ly Child of Beth-le-hem, de-scend to__ us, we pray;

a-bove thy deep and dream-less sleep the si-lent__ stars go by:
while mor-tals sleep, the an-gels keep their watch of__ won-d'ring love.
So God im-parts to hu-man hearts the bless-ings__ of His heav'n.
cast out our sin and en-ter in; be born in__ us to-day.

yet in thy dark streets shin-eth the ev-er-last-ing Light:
O morn-ing stars, to-geth-er pro-claim the ho-ly birth!
No ear may hear His com-ing, but in this world of sin,
We hear the Christ-mas an-gels the great glad tid-ings tell;

the hopes and fears of all the years are met in thee to-night.
And prais-es sing to God the King, and peace to men on earth.
where meek souls will re-ceive Him still, the dear Christ en-ters in.
O come to us, a-bide with us, our Lord Em-man-u-el.

TEXT: Cecil F. Alexander || b. 1818, Redcross, Wicklow, Ireland
d. October 12, 1895, Londonderry, Ireland

Cecil Alexander started writing poetry as a child for her school journal. As an adult, she published some of her poetry in *Dublin University Magazine* under pseudonyms. Her poem "Burial of Moses" caused Alfred Lord Tennyson to say it was one of the few poems by another author he wished he had written. She wrote over 400 poems and hymns that were mostly for children. This poem was written to explain and amplify the line from the Apostle's Creed, "who was conceived by the Holy Spirit, born of the virgin Mary." It was first published in her book titled *Hymns for Little Children,* but included the label, "suitable also for adults." Every year since 1919, the Kings College Chapel in Cambridge, England, has used this as a processional hymn for their famous Festival of Lessons and Carols. Another hymn of Alexander's that is greatly loved is "All Things Bright and Beautiful."

TUNE: Henry J. Gauntlett || b. July 9, 1805, Wellington, Shropshire, England
d. February 21, 1876, London, England

Henry J. Gauntlett wrote the tune for this poem. He was a gifted nineteenth-century English musician, but also a lawyer, author, organ designer, and organ recitalist. The tune first appeared in his book *Christmas Carols,* published in 1849. The name IRBY is the name of a village in Lincolnshire, England.

As you sing this hymn . . . you begin with a creedal declaration of what Christians believe about Jesus. It is a kind of theological sermon. But in the third stanza, you declare what these truths mean to you personally. He is your pattern for life. He is a friend who understands your feelings of weakness or helplessness, your fears and tears, and who joins in when you are glad. Best of all, you declare in the final stanza that someday Christians will meet Him! Because of His redeeming love, this One whom we think of at Christmas as merely a child has ascended to heaven to prepare our eternal home with Him.

Our world is quite confused about Christmas. Santa Claus has become, for many, the image of Christmas. In a sermon, pastor John MacArthur pointed out that Santa has been given almost God-like qualities—able to visit every home in the entire world in a single night, knowing when you've been bad or good, and worst of all, he judges your works, giving gifts to good people and coal to bad people! Though imaginary, Santa is honored and exalted.[26] While people know this is a fable, it reveals the subtle change from the power of truth to the power of make-believe.

The true and living spirit of Christmas is found in the only perfect One who came down from the glories of heaven to the lowest position on earth. It is unmerited grace that offers His gifts to all those who seek His forgiveness and accept His love. If you are a child, this beautiful Christmas hymn speaks to you and for you. It should be one of the Christmas carols you know and love the best because its truth will be your hope for the rest of your life. If you are an adult, let it refocus your worship and help form a Christmas theology of what you believe and celebrate during this season.

Once in Royal David's City

16

Christ Jesus . . . though he was in the form of God . . .
emptied himself, by taking the form of a servant,
being born in the likeness of men.

PHILIPPIANS 2:5–7

IRBY
Text: Cecil F. Alexander
Music: Henry J. Gauntlett

1. Once in roy - al Da - vid's cit - y stood a low - ly cat - tle
2. He came down to earth from heav - en Who is God and Lord of
3. Je - sus is our child - hood's pat - tern, day by day like us He
4. And our eyes at last shall see Him, through His own re - deem - ing

shed, where a moth - er laid her ba - by in a
all, and His shel - ter was a sta - ble, and His
grew, He was lit - tle, weak, and help - less, tears and
love; for that Child, so dear and gen - tle, is our

man - ger for His bed: Ma - ry was that moth - er
cra - dle was a stall: with the poor and meek and
smiles like us He knew: and He feels for all our
Lord in heav'n a - bove, and He leads His chil - dren

mild, Je - sus Christ her lit - tle child.
low - ly lived on earth, our Sav - ior ho - ly.
sad - ness, and He shares in all our glad - ness.
on to the place where He is gone.

TEXT AND TUNE: Keith and Kristyn
Getty and Stuart Townend

b. December 16, 1974, Lisburn, Northern Ireland
b. May 22, 1980, Belfast, Northern Ireland
b. June 1, 1963, West Yorkshire, England

This hymn is one of the earliest collaborations by the writing team of Keith and Kristyn Getty and Stuart Townend, a new generation of hymn writers from the United Kingdom who follow the musical heritage of Watts, Wesley, and Newton. All were raised in Christian homes. Townend's advanced education in literature is evidenced in the quality of his poetry. He resides in England and is a worship leader and composer. He writes: "Songs remain in the mind in a way sermons do not, so songwriters have an important role and a huge responsibility."[27] Keith Getty's advanced education is in music. He was honored in June 2017 as an "Officer of the Order of the British Empire" by Queen Elizabeth II for his contribution to music and modern hymn writing. Keith was introduced to Kristyn by his friend and her uncle, a professor at Oxford University. They were married in 2004, and they split their time between Belfast and Nashville.

This team of modern hymn writers contribute on multiple levels to a sort of re-inventing of the traditional hymn form that crosses classical, folk, and contemporary styles. They have written sixty of the most popular two thousand hymns in America and the United Kingdom, according to the Christian Copywriting Licensing. The Gettys tour the US extensively, and their Christmas tour includes Carnegie Hall and most of the major concert halls across the country.

As you sing this hymn . . . you find in the title the unique focus of thought describing these few words by the gospel writer John: "From the fullness of His grace we have all received." These words portray the inestimable value Jesus brought through His incarnation. Consider the rich couplets of adjectives that permeate the stanzas: human frailty, meanest worth, holy innocent, joy unspeakable.

He was despised, rejected, and crushed for the sins past, present, and future of the world. "This is the wonder of Jesus." But it is the word "fullness" that reveals the richest treasure of deity inserted into humanity. There is an inexhaustible supply of what the world needs—grace, hope, and God Himself. No amount of good deeds are full of enough goodness. No amount of right living provides adequate righteousness. To attempt to earn grace is futile and negates the power of the incarnation.

We not only need grace for our salvation but also in our living. The great English preacher, Charles Spurgeon, wrote profoundly about "fullness."

> There is fullness of blessings of every sort and shape; a fullness of grace to pardon, of grace to regenerate, of grace to sanctify, of grace to preserve and to perfect. There is fullness at all times; a fullness of comfort in affliction, a fullness of guidance in prosperity. A fullness of every divine attribute, of wisdom, of power, of love. A fullness which is impossible to survey, much less explore. Fullness there must be when the stream is always flowing, and yet the well springs up as free, as rich, as full as ever. Come, believer, and get all your needs supplied; ask largely, and you shall receive largely, for this "fullness" is inexhaustible and is stored where all the needy may reach it, even in Jesus, Immanuel—God with us.[28]

We say it again: Come, believer, and get all your needs supplied!

Fullness of Grace

17

For from his fullness we have all received, grace upon grace. For the law was given through Moses; grace and truth came through Jesus Christ.

JOHN 1:16–17

Text: Keith and Kristyn Getty, Stuart Townend
Music: Keith and Kristyn Getty, Stuart Townend

1. Full - ness of grace in man's hu - man frail - ty; this is the won-der of
2. Full - ness of grace, the love of the Fa - ther shown in the face___ of
3. Full - ness of hope in Christ we had longed_ for, prom - ise of God_ in

Je - sus. Lay - ing a - side His pow - er and glo - ry,
Je - sus. Stoop - ing to bear the weight of hu - man - i - ty,
Je - sus. Through His o - be - dience we are for - giv - en,

hum - bly He en - tered our world. Chose the_ path of_ mean - est_worth;
walk - ing the Cal - va - ry road. Christ, the_ ho - ly_ In - no - cent,
o - p'ning the flood-gates of heav'n. All our_hopes and_ dreams we_ bring

scan - dal_ of a_ vir - gin birth. Born in a sta - ble,
took our_ sin and_ pun - ish-ment. Full - ness of God, de -
glad - ly_ as an_ of - fer- ing. Full - ness of life and

cold and re - jec - ted: Here lies the hope_ of the world.
spised and re - ject - ed: Crushed for the sins_ of the world.
joy un - speak - a - ble: God's gift in love_ to the world.

December 12   Thou Who Wast Rich Beyond All Splendor

TEXT: Frank Houghton   ‖   b. 1894, Stafford, Staffordshire, England
                                d. January 25, 1972, Kent, England

Frank Houghton was an Anglican missionary, bishop, and author. He was educated at London University and ordained to the ministry in 1917. After holding pastoral positions in England, he went to China with the China Inland Mission (CIM). He became general director of the mission in 1940, but in 1951, the mission was forced to leave China. He returned to England and served as a vicar and later the editorial secretary of CIM.

In 1934, civil war between Chinese government forces and the Communist Red Army had begun making it a difficult and dangerous time for missionaries; some had been captured and imprisoned. One young couple, John and Betty Stam, had been killed by the Red Army. News of their deaths shocked and saddened the entire mission. When word of the terrible incident reached CIM headquarters in Shanghai, Houghton decided to make a trip throughout the country to visit the mission outposts, even though it was risky. While traveling over the mountains of Szechwan, Houghton was reminded of 2 Corinthians 8:9: "For you know the grace of our Lord Jesus Christ, that though he was rich, yet for your sakes, he became poor, so that you by his poverty might become rich." These words, impressed into his mind, resulted in this beautiful, powerful, and comforting poem.

TUNE: French Carol Melody   ‖

QUELLE EST CETTE ODEUR AGREABLE (translated: "Whence is that goodly fragrance flowing?") is a seventeenth-century French Christmas carol about the nativity. The origin of the tune is unknown. The tune made its way from France to England. In 1782, the tune was used by John Gay in his famous *The Beggar's Opera*. It was later matched with Houghton's poem.

As you sing this hymn . . . note the word *beyond*—the fifth word in all three stanzas. Each time Houghton is pointing to something *beyond* our comprehension: the splendor of heaven, the wonder of the Trinity, and the extent of Christ's love for us. We can comprehend, on some level, what it means to be poor. Try to discover all the short descriptions of what Jesus gave up or brought to us. "Thrones for a manger" is one example. There are at least four more!

And the fact that Jesus would leave one extreme for the other leads to only one conclusion: He is worthy of our highest commitment ("Emmanuel, within us dwelling"), our complete trust ("make us what Thou would'st have us be"), and our deepest adoration ("Savior and King, we worship Thee"). Indeed, it was because missionaries like the Stams knew this Christ and His love that they could give their all, including their very lives.

We sometimes hear about benevolent wealthy people who are willing to share their riches for various needs around the world. But have you ever heard of a millionaire or billionaire who gave away everything they owned and became homeless themselves? That is what Jesus did. "The Son of man has no place to lay his head" (Luke 9:58). But He owned the universe! The last six words must be our response: "Savior and King, we worship Thee."

Thou Who Wast Rich Beyond All Splendor 18

For you know the grace of our Lord Jesus Christ,
that though he was rich, yet for your sake he became poor,
so that you by his poverty might become rich.

2 CORINTHIANS 8:9

QUELLE EST CETTE ODEUR AGREABLE
Text: Frank Houghton
Music: French carol melody

1. Thou Who wast rich be - yond all splen - dor,
2. Thou Who art God be - yond all prais - ing,
3. Thou Who art love be - yond all tell - ing,

all for love's sake be - cam - est poor;
all for love's sake be - cam - est man;
Sav - ior and King, we wor - ship Thee.

thrones for a man - ger didst sur - ren - der,
stoop - ing so low, but sin - ners rais - ing,
Em - man - u - el, with - in us dwell - ing,

sap - phire - paved courts for sta - ble floor.
heav'n - ward by Thine e - ter - nal plan.
make us what Thou wouldst have us be.

Thou Who wast rich be - yond all splen - dor,
Thou Who art God be - yond all prais - ing,
Thou Who art Love be yond all tell - ing,

all for love's sake be - cam - est poor.
all for love's sake be - cam - est man.
Sa - vior and King, we wor - ship Thee.

December 13 What Child Is This?

TEXT: Traditional English Carol || b. June 14, 1837, Bristol, England
Adapted, William Chatterton Dix   d. September 9, 1898, Cheddar, Somerset, England

William Dix's father gave his son the middle name Chatterton after one of his heroes, Thomas Chatterton, an English poet. And he encouraged his son to follow after his namesake. Dix studied poets and poetry, read classic literature, and spent time in college focusing on his writing. Although he became the manager of a marine insurance company, Dix made time to write. When illness caused him to be bedridden for months, he wrote a lengthy poem, "The Manger Throne," the story of the men from the East who came to visit the baby Jesus (Matt. 2:1–12). The text is written from their perspective, which is why it is in the "Epiphany" section of this hymnal (see "As with Gladness Men of Old"). The poem was published and quickly became popular in England and America, where the Civil War was just ending. An unknown Englishman put the words of the poem to the beautiful English folk song GREENSLEEVES, creating this carol.

TUNE: English Melody, 16th c. ||

GREENSLEEVES is an English folk melody of uncertain origin, dating back to the sixteenth century. Some attribute it to King Henry VIII as a gift to Anne Boleyn, but for reasons based on style, that is not likely. In Shakespeare's *The Merry Wives of Windsor*, written around 1602, one character calls out, "Let the sky rain potatoes; let it thunder to the tune of 'Greensleeves'!" It is truly one of the most hauntingly beautiful tunes ever written, and "What Child Is This?" is the reason it is well-known to this day.

As you sing this hymn . . . notice that the first two stanzas ask two profound questions, "Who?" and "Why?" The first, "What child is this?" is rhetorical, a way of asking, "who is this one?" Although you know the answer, you sing as an expression of wonder and awe, a way of saying, "this appears too good to be true!" Is this baby on Mary's lap really Christ the King? The "why?" follows: Why would God in Jesus come to earth "in such mean estate" (a lowly place)? And why would "nails, spear . . . pierce him through"? A false view of Christmas expects Christmas songs to be only lullabies of happy thoughts. Think of secular Christmas songs. While a few are melancholy, can you think of any that speak of death or tragedies?

We understand the nativity is only the beginning of the story. We cannot stop at the stable. David Mathis writes: "The light and joy of Christmas are hollow at best, and even horrifying if we sever the link between Bethlehem and Golgotha . . . 'Nails, spears shall pierce him through' doesn't ruin Christmas. It gives the season its power."[29]

The third stanza describes the right response: offer your highest treasures, enthrone Him as reigning Lord, and raise songs of praise. In short, this carol is a Q&A—a question and answer concerning a matter of more importance than all other mysteries in our universe. In a sermon, Pastor Richard Phillips declared, "Our response must be far more than a little cultural observation. It calls us to our greatest life commitment."[30] Which response have you made?

What Child Is This?

They saw the child with Mary his mother,
and they fell down and worshiped him.
Then, opening their treasures, they offered him gifts.

MATTHEW 2:11

GREENSLEEVES
Text: Traditional English carol
Adapt. William C. Dix
Music: English melody, 16th c.

1. What Child is this,— Who, laid to rest,— on Mar-y's lap— is
2. Why lies He in— such mean es-tate,—where ox and ass— are
3. So bring Him in-cense, gold, and myrrh:—come peas-ant, king,— to

sleep - ing? Whom an-gels greet— with an-thems sweet,— while
feed - ing? Good Chris-tian, fear;— for sin-ners here— the
own Him; the King of kings— sal-va-tion brings,— let

shep - herds watch— are keep - ing? This, this— is
si - lent Word— is plead - ing. Nails, spear,— shall
lov - ing hearts— en-throne Him. Raise, raise— the

Christ the King,—Whom shep-herds guard— and an-gels sing:
pierce Him through; the cross be borne— for me, for you:
song on high,— the vir-gin sings— her lul-la-by:

haste, haste— to bring Him laud, the Babe,— the son— of Mar - y.
hail, hail— the Word made flesh, the Babe,— the son— of Mar - y.
joy, joy— for Christ is born, the Babe,— the son— of Mar - y.

TEXT AND TUNE: Traditional Appalachian
Text and Melody
Adapted and arranged, John Jacob Niles

b. April 28, 1892, Louisville, Kentucky
d. March 1, 1980, Lexington, Kentucky

John Jacob Niles was born into a musical family with a great-grandfather who was a composer, an organist, and a cello manufacturer! Niles learned music theory from his mother, and at a young age, he was inspired to collect folk music from the hills of Kentucky. Eventually, Niles enrolled in the Cincinnati Conservatory, from which a professional career in music began. From Chicago to New York, from the opera house to the nightclub, he performed and perfected his trademark style of folk singing. His concerts and recordings of traditional mountain and African American material brought great acclaim. From this material, two Christmas songs grew to be his most well-known: "Jesus, Jesus, Rest Your Head" and "I Wonder as I Wander."

Niles's own words written on an album tell the remarkable story of this carol:

"I Wonder as I Wander" grew out of three lines of music sung for me by a girl who called herself Annie Morgan—a tousled, unwashed blond, and very lovely. She sang the first three lines of a verse. Introducing myself, I asked her about the song. All she knew about it was that her mother had taught it to her and her grandmother taught it to her mother. At twenty-five cents a performance, I tried to get her to sing all the song. After eight tries . . . I had only three lines of verse, a garbled fragment of melodic material—and a magnificent idea. With the writing of additional verses and the development of the original melodic material, "I Wonder as I Wander"came into being. I sang it for five years in my concerts before it caught on. Since then, it has been sung by soloists and choral groups wherever the English language is spoken and sung.[31]

As you sing this hymn . . . it demands to be sung simply and quietly. The melody is haunting, and you can easily picture someone wandering alone at night, looking at the stars, and asking: Why did Jesus come? Why for "on'ry" people? (Some versions change the otherwise understood "ornery" to "ordinary.") Why die for them? These are common questions for anyone who has not met the Savior. On a human level, the story of Christmas resulting in Good Friday does not make sense! The questions are not answered in the carol.

Only because of Easter does the death of Jesus makes sense. His sacrificial death would be meaningless had He not risen from the dead. The colloquial term "on'ry people" reaches to the heart of it. We are sinful and condemned people. "Ordinary" is not strong enough. Without Him, we are doomed. John 3:17 makes it clear: "For God did not send his Son into the world to condemn the world, but so that the world might be saved through him." Perhaps you have wondered, is this all true? Perhaps you even want to believe but you simply don't understand. If so, you are like Nicodemus who came to Jesus one night and asked what he must do to be saved. Read Jesus' answer to him in "Christmas in the Bible," #32–35.

Jesus used the language of birth when He told Nicodemus that he must be "born again." You too must have a "nativity" of your soul. If you have not already, make this Christmas the beginning of your life! Cry out, "Hosanna, Lord Jesus!" He will save you.

I Wonder as I Wander

20

The people who walked in darkness
have seen a great light.

ISAIAH 9:2

Text: Traditional Appalachian carol, adpt. John Jacob Niles
Music: Traditional American melody, arr. John Jacob Niles

1. I won-der as I wan-der, out un-der the sky, how Je-sus the Sav-ior did come for to die for poor o-n'ry peo-ple like you and like I; I won-der as I wan-der, out un-der the sky.

2. When Ma-ry birthed Je-sus 'twas in a cow's stall, with wise men and farm-ers and shep-herds and all, but high from God's heav-en a star's light did fall, the prom-ise of a-ges it then did re-call.

3. If Je-sus had want-ed for an-y wee thing, a star in the sky or a bird on the wing, or all of God's an-gels in heav'n for to sing, He sure-ly could have it, 'cause He was the King.

4. I won-der as I wan-der, out un-der the sky, how Je-sus the Sav-ior did come for to die for poor o-n'ry peo-ple like you and like I; I won-der as I wan-der, out un-der the sky.

61

December 15   Good Christian Men, Rejoice!

TEXT: Heinrich Seuse   b. 1295, Germany
English paraphrase by John Mason Neale, 1853   d. 1366, Germany

The origin of this fourteenth-century carol is credited to a German mystic and Dominican monk named Heinrich Seuse. A legend claims that Seuse heard angels sing these words and actually joined them in a dance of worship. The famous modern English composer, John Rutter, created a delightful short opera-like presentation of that legend in a composition called "Brother Heinrich's Christmas." In this fairy tale, the monk's pet donkey helped him remember the angels' melody for a new song at the monks' special Christmas Eve service. If indeed, it was first performed for monks, the first line and title directed to men is logical. Even though some modern versions change it to "Christians *all*, rejoice," we also understand the word "men" to include all humanity.

It was John Mason Neale who made the carol known to the English-speaking world through the English paraphrase we sing today. Neale was an Anglican pastor with great skills of translating. He gave us "Of the Father's Love Begotten," and for a children's hymnal, he created the unusual carol, "Good King Wenceslas."

TUNE: Traditional German Melody, 14th c.

How can a tune last over 600 years and continue to be a favorite of carols we sing at Christmas? When the tune is eminently singable and has an inherent feeling of joy and dance. Even though IN DULCI JUBILO is centered around only five notes, it is so beautiful that many great composers used it in their extended compositions, including Dietrich Buxtehude, Michael Praetorius, J. S. Bach, Franz Liszt, and Gustav Holst. Yet we do not know who wrote it. Ironically, the transcription by Thomas Helmore included a mistake. But when Neale created the English version, he followed the notational error by including the repeated words, "News, news," "Joy, joy," and "Peace, Peace." Some editions leave this measure out, but we believe it makes the tune unique and memorable and that these are fitting one-word exclamations of exultation.

As you sing this hymn . . . even if sung without accompaniment, you can feel it dance. It is the very musical language of the words rejoice or joy! The joy is found in every part of our being—heart, soul, and voice. The expression of "endless bliss" might sound excessive if we didn't recall that the salvation takes us to the "everlasting hall"—to heaven. This joy is not just about the birth of a baby but the result!

In a sermon, J. Ligon Duncan offered this interesting take on the animals: "I think the first stanza is designed to be an irony. . . . Yes, heaven and earth ought to be surrounding him and bowing down, but that wasn't happening at the birth. There may have been some oxen and donkeys bowing down, but none of the great people of the earth. It's another one of those ironies of the Messiah's condition."[32]

The angels told the shepherds that they had "tidings of *great joy*!" The wise men were "overjoyed" or "shouted joyfully." There is no sadness like death. But you "need not fear the grave." As you meditate on and sing this beautiful carol, let it soak into your heart and soul with the lasting joy of the knowledge of your salvation that comes through Jesus. He "calls you one, and calls you all."

Good Christian Men, Rejoice!

21

Sing aloud, O daughter of Zion;
shout, O Israel!
Rejoice and exult with all your heart,
O daughter of Jerusalem!

ZEPHANIAH 3:14

IN DULCI JUBILO
Text: Heinrich Seuse, Tr. John Mason Neale
Music: Traditional German Melody, 14th c.

1. Good Christ-ian men, re - joice____ with heart and soul and voice!____
2. Good Christ-ian men, re - joice____ with heart and soul and voice!____
3. Good Christ-ian men, re - joice____ with heart and soul and voice!____

Give ye heed to what we say: News! News! Je - sus Christ is born to-day!
Now ye hear of end-less bliss: Joy! Joy! Je - sus Christ was born for this!
Now ye need not fear the grave: Peace! Peace! Je - sus Christ was born to save!

Ox and ass be - fore Him bow, and He is in the man - ger now:
He has o - pened heav - en's door, and we are blest for - ev - er more.
Calls you one and calls you all to gain His ev - er - last - ing hall.

Christ is born to - day!____ Christ is born to - day!____
Christ was born for this!____ Christ was born for this!____
Christ was born to save!____ Christ was born to save!____

TEXT: George Ratcliffe Woodward ‖ b. December 27, 1848, Cheshire, England
d. March 3, 1934, London, England

A graduate of Cambridge University, George Woodward served as a curate, a vicar, and a rector in the Church of England. Along with pastoral duties, he wrote religious verse. He frequently collaborated with composer Charles Wood. In 1924, together they published *A Cambridge Carol Book: Fifty-Two Songs for Christmas, Easter, and Other Seasons.* In this carol, Woodward employed the macaronic style—a mixture of languages. The words "i-o, i-o, i-o" are a Latin expression of joy, similar to our word "Hooray!" *Hosanna in Excelsis* means "highest praise." "Matin chimes" are bells played in the morning.

TUNE: Jehan Tabourot (1519–1593) ‖ b. June 15, 1866, Vicar's Hill, Ireland
Harmonized by Charles Wood ‖ d. July 12, 1926, Cambridge, England

The melody of this carol was a dance tune composed by Jehan Tabourot (1519–1593) and named BRANLE DE L'OFFICIAL. Woodward paired it with his text, and Wood harmonized it for *A Cambridge Carol Book.* It is considered one of the most explicit examples of the Christmas carol as dance. Wood was an Irish composer and teacher. His students included the great composers Ralph Vaughan Williams of Cambridge and Herbert Howells of the Royal College of Music.

As you sing this hymn . . . you are expressing pure joy, and ideally, the same holy joy exuded by the angels to the shepherds. Is it scriptural that in heaven there were "bells ringing"? Not precisely. But Jesus tells us "there will be more joy in heaven over one sinner who repents. . . . joy before the angels of God over one sinner who repents" (Luke 15:7, 10). Certainly, there was joy in heaven when Jesus was born, as the angels knew what it would mean to all the world. Historically, bells are associated with religious rituals, and steeple bells would call communities together for church services. Bells are also used to commemorate important events. At the declaration of peace at the end of WWII, bells rang for hours and hours throughout England.

In this dancing carol, you'll find the title of this book, *Hosanna in Excelsis.* The original Aramaic use of the word hosanna meant "please save," as a cry for deliverance. But as a liturgical expression, it has come to serve as a cry of joy and praise for deliverance granted or anticipated. Through Jesus, the words, "Lord, save us," have become, "Praise God and His Messiah, we *are* saved!" It is a three-word doxology. It is like a bell ringing with the declaration of 1 Peter 1:8: "Though you do not now see him, you believe in him and rejoice with joy that is inexpressible and filled with glory."

But be prepared. The word "Gloria" in the refrain is a long melisma (many notes on one syllable). It is something choirs or soloists do often, but not congregations. But you can do it! First, take a deep breath and then try to sustain the "glo-" all the way through in one breath. But try not to snicker if you don't make it. You can certainly take a breath anywhere. Think of it as a metaphor for how long we should be thanking and praising God.

Ding, Dong! Merrily on High

*I bring you good news of great joy
that will be for all the people.*

LUKE 2:10

BRANLE DE L'OFFICIAL
Text: George Ratcliffe Woodward
Music: Jehan Tabourot, Adpt. Charles Wood

1. Ding, dong! Mer-ri-ly on high, in heav'n the bells are ring - ing.
2. E'en so, here be-low, be - low, let stee-ple bells be swung - en,
3. Pray you, du-ti-ful-ly prime your ma-tin chime, you ring - ers;

Ding, dong! Ve-ri-ly the sky is riv'n with an-gels sing - ing!
and "i - o, i - o, i - o!" by priest and peo-ple sung - en!
may you beau-ti-ful-ly rhyme your ev'n-time song, you sing - ers.

Glo - - - - - - - - - - - - - - - - - - ri - a, Ho-san-na in Ex-cel - sis!

Glo - - - - - - - - - - - - - - - - - - ri - a, Ho-san-na in Ex-cel - sis!

TEXT: Henry Wadsworth Longfellow   ‖   b. February 27, 1807, Portland, Maine
                                          d. March 24, 1882, Cambridge, Massachusetts

Longfellow was a child prodigy, beginning school at age three, reading classical literature, and writing poems by age six. By nineteen, he had graduated from college and was made a professor of modern language at Bowdoin College. Soon he was a professor at Harvard University. At only twenty-seven, Longfellow was already one of America's most respected scholars. With a loving wife and a beautiful home overlooking the Charles River, life was good—at least until his wife became ill and died. He remarried seven years later, and he and his second wife had five children. Longfellow achieved great wealth and fame and honorary doctorates from Oxford and Cambridge. His second wife died tragically while she was lighting candles and her clothes caught fire. In an attempt to put out the fire, Longfellow was severely burned; from then on, he wore a full beard to conceal the scars on his face. On the heels of this personal tragedy, the Civil War began. Longfellow hated war, and this one hit even closer to home when, without his permission, Longfellow's son enlisted, only to eventually be severely injured.

By 1862, Longfellow's once wonderful world was upside down. On Christmas 1863, he wrote the poem "Christmas Bells," which became this carol. It was a dark poem, and were it not for the final stanza, it would be absent of any hope. Two original, deleted stanzas speak of cannons with "black, accursed mouth," rending the continent like an earthquake and drowning out "peace on Earth."[33] But in the pealing of church bells, Longfellow was reminded there is a living God. Though we do not know the depth of his religious convictions, God restored hope through what Longfellow knew the church proclaimed.

TUNE: John Baptiste Calkin   ‖   b. March 16, 1827, London, England
                                     d. May 15, 1905, Islington, London, England

John Baptiste Calkin was born into a musical family and was taught by his father. He wrote much for the organ, including numerous transcriptions, and he scored many string arrangements, as well as original sonatas. Yet, were it not for the decision to write a tune for Longfellow's poem ten years after it was published, we might never have heard of Calkin or any of his music.

As you sing this hymn . . . there may be circumstances in your life causing you to fully identify with the words "in despair I bowed my head." Life can be so cruel that bells or the music of Christmas do not bring any joy. But God places something far better than bells in our lives when our peace is gone. His Holy Word will ring clear with words of comfort, direction, hope, and promises. Do not listen to the world's music. Instead of bells, it may sound sirens. Instead of assurances of God's love for you, it will tell you a lie that "there is no peace on earth." As you sing this hymn, let the testimony of a broken poet from over a hundred years ago remind you and encourage you that God is not dead or asleep! Take heart. The Christmas message of the angels is for you, and the Prince of Peace is singing to you.

I Heard the Bells on Christmas Day

23

For to us a child is born . . .
and his name shall be called Wonderful Counselor,
Mighty God, Everlasting Father, Prince of Peace.

ISAIAH 9:6

WALTHAM
Text: Henry W. Longfellow
Music: John Calkin

1. I heard the bells on Christ - mas day their old, fa - mil - iar
2. I thought how, as the day had come, the bel - fries of all
3. And in de - spair I bowed my head; "There is no peace on
4. Then pealed the bells more loud and deep: "God is not dead, nor
5. Till ring - ing, sing - ing on its way, the world re - volved from

car - ols play, and wild and sweet the words re - peat of
Christ - en - dom had rolled a - long the un - brok - ken song of
earth," I said; "For hate is strong, and mocks the song of
doth He sleep; the wrong shall fail, the right pre - vail, with
night to day, a voice, a chime, a chant su - blime of

peace on earth, good will to men.
peace on earth, good will to men.
peace on earth, good will to men."
peace on earth, good will to men."
peace on earth, good will to men.

TEXT AND TUNE: English Carol, 18th c.

When this carol was written, you would not have heard it in church. That is because, for its day, it was much too frivolous and happy! The church music of the eighteenth century, even at Christmas, was somber, slow, and for some, far too severe for real celebration. It is possible this was written in rebellion—not to be sung in church, but in the streets or homes of believers who saw the birthday of Christ as a time for joyous celebration. Since no name is associated with either the text or the tune, perhaps they felt safer in anonymity.

Some suggest that the word "merry" is better translated "mighty." We do not agree, and research reveals no time when the word merry was employed to describe strength. A brief study of English literature from Shakespeare, Shelley, or Tennyson employs phrases such as "rest you fair," "rest you happy," and "rest myself content." The somewhat archaic couplet "rest you" is similar in use to our modern expression, "rest assured" or "rest easy." It is the placement of the comma after the word "merry" and not after "you" that clarifies this entreaty of joy to people who may be in dismay. Charles Dickens employed this song in his great story *A Christmas Carol*. But it was too much for Scrooge, who rejected it and all it proclaimed.

As you sing this hymn . . . it could be the most encouraging and uplifting song of your season! Rather than being a song about coming home for Christmas, or Santa's visit, or trips in a sleigh, here, you are singing of your encounter with the One by whom all dismay and fear and sadness is conquered. This is not a vertically directed lyric of praise. It is a horizontal entreaty to "be of good cheer" with much more than merely positive thinking. The repeating refrain proclaims the two pillars of blessings—comfort for our sorrow and pain, and joy for our sadness and misery.

So consider an old tradition that is seldom done today: recruit another family and go caroling in your neighborhood. Or sing at your office party or at a senior living home. From this hymnal, choose the songs and stanzas you have most easily committed to memory and share the joy. You never know who will hear you or who is living in "dismay" or is sadly "astray." Your gift of song may be what is needed for sad souls.

God Rest You Merry, Gentlemen

24

*Fear not, for behold,
I bring you good news of great joy
that will be for all the people.*

LUKE 2:10

Text: English carol, 18th c.
Music: English melody

1. God rest you mer - ry, gen - tle - men, let noth - ing you dis - may! Re -
2. From God our heav'n-ly Fa - ther a bless - ed an - gel came; and
3. "Fear not," then said the an - gel, "let noth - ing you af - fright; to
4. Now to the Lord sing prai - ses all you with - in this place! With

mem - ber Christ our Sav - ior was born on Christ-mas day, to
un - to cer - tain shep - herds brought tid - ings of the same: how
you is born a Sav - ior in Da - vid's town to - night, to
Christ-ian love and broth - er - hood each o - ther now em - brace, this

save us all from Sa - tan's pow'r when we were gone a -
that in Beth - le - hem was born the Son of God by
free all those who trust in Him from Sa - tan's pow'r and
ho - ly tide of Christ - mas all oth - ers doth de -

stray; O____ tid - ings of com - fort and joy, com-fort and
name.
might."
face.

joy, O____ tid - ings of com - fort and joy.

December 19 On Christmas Night All Christians Sing

TEXT: Traditional English Carol ‖

This text is known in Great Britain as "Sussex Carol." It was first published in 1864 by Luke Wadding, a seventeenth-century Irish bishop. It is not known whether he wrote it or merely copied it from an earlier writing. The text was rediscovered over 200 years later by musicologists in England who were studying the folk music of Great Britain. Cecil Sharp (1859–1924), the leader of the folklore revival in England, is responsible for finding, writing down, and preserving much of the folk music and traditional dances of that culture. Here, he restored and kept for us one of the most joyous of Christmas poems.

TUNE: English Folk Tune
Adapted by Ralph Vaughan Williams ‖

The tune is also a folk song from England. The famous musicologist and composer of the early twentieth century, Ralph Vaughan Williams, heard the song sung by Harriet Verrall at Monk's Gate in Sussex, England. He wrote it down, arranged it, and published it in 1919, under the name SUSSEX CAROL. It is a favorite carol in Great Britain and is regularly used at Cambridge in the King's College Service of Nine Lessons and Carols.

As you sing this hymn . . . have you noticed a recurring theme in so many carols of Christmas? Gladness, joy, merriment! Often, even without words, the tunes convey these emotions. SUSSEX CAROL sparkles with joy and the "news of great mirth." So the text appropriately asks, "Why should all on earth be sad, since our Redeemer made us glad?"

Sometimes people find Christmas to be a difficult time because they are lonely or have painful memories that still cause grief, especially if there has been a recent loss of a loved one. Many people say their stress level increases during the holiday season, commonly due to lack of time and money, commercialism, the pressures of gift-giving, and family gatherings.

If you are in this place, these rich carols will offer hope. The third stanza of this hymn says that by the grace of God, the results of sin can be replaced with "life and health." Depression too can put us in a place of emotional darkness. But the fourth stanza, quoting John 1:5, declares that Jesus is light for darkness: "The light shines in the darkness, and the darkness has not overcome it." John 8:12 says "whoever follows me will not walk in darkness, but will have the light of life." Turn to "Christmas in the Bible," #31. These truths in poetry have provided encouragement and joy to hundreds of thousands of people before you. May they also speak life and light to you this very day.

If you are singing this carol as a family or in a group, you may add to the joyous experience by dividing into two groups. One group sings the first phrase, and the other echoes the repeated phrase. Then both groups sing together the last two phrases of each stanza. Employ a quicker tempo in order to experience the joyful mood of the carol text. And remember, be glad—not sad!

On Christmas Night All Christians Sing   25

*The angel said to them, "Do not be afraid.
I bring you good news of great joy
that will be for all the people."*

LUKE 2:10

SUSSEX CAROL
Text: Traditional English carol
Music: English Folk Song, Adpt. Ralph Vaughan Williams

1. On Christ - mas night all Christ - ians sing, to hear the news_ the
2. Then why should all on earth_ be sad, since our Re - deem - er
3. When sin de - parts be - fore_ His grace, then life and health come
4. All out of dark - ness we_ have light, which made the an - gels

an - gels bring; on Christ - mas night all Christ - ians sing, to
made us glad, then why should all on earth_ be sad, since
in its place; when sin de - parts be - fore_ His grace, then
sing this night; all out of dark - ness we_ have light, which

hear the news____ the an - gels bring:
our Re - deem - er made us glad,
life and health____ come in its place;
made the an - gels sing this night:

news of great joy,____ news of____ great mirth,
when from our sin____ He set____ us free,
heav - en and earth____ with joy____ may sing,
"Glo - ry to God____ and peace_ to men,

news of our mer - ci - ful_ King's birth.____
all for to gain our lib - er - ty?____
all for to see the new - born King,____
now and for - ev - er - more. A - men."____

December 20   Infant Holy, Infant Lowly

TEXT: Polish Carol ‖

This ancient Polish carol is of unknown origin. First published in 1908, it was translated into English thirteen years later in 1921 by Edith Reed (1885–1933). Reed worked as an associate for the Royal College of Organists in London and was the editor of its music magazine, *Music and Youth*, in which the carol appeared.

TUNE: Traditional Polish Melody ‖

The composer of the tune W ZLOBIE LEZY is also unknown. The name is Polish for "in a manger lies." It follows the rhythmic pattern of a *mazurka*, a Polish folk dance in triple meter. Two eighth notes precede two quarter notes, with the accent on the second beat, the first quarter note. This entire melody follows this pattern, occurring sixteen times. (The famous Polish composer Frederick Chopin made mazurkas well-known to the Polish ear, having composed fifty-seven of them.)

As you sing this hymn . . . imagine you are watching a painting of a crèche in progress. Each time the rhythmic pattern repeats, it is like the brushstroke of a painter, adding a new aspect of the picture.

First and foremost, in the very center, lies the infant in a cattle stall. He is surrounded by animals, which you can almost smell and hear. Above the manger, there are cherubic angels flying overhead. Through a window, you see on a nearby hillside the sleeping shepherds with their flocks of sheep. They are suddenly awakened by the glorious song of the angels. Now the painting is placed in a frame, and a plaque on the bottom reads, "Christ the babe is Lord of all."

But the second stanza paints a slightly different picture—one that you are in. As you look at the shepherds and get a grasp of the glory that was revealed to them, you begin to rejoice. You are "free from sorrow" and "voice praises" as you greet a new day. Why? "Christ the babe was born for you." Amazingly, this is a painting that has you in mind.

Although the story of Christmas cannot be reduced to a two-dimensional painting, it helps to picture the gospel in its simplest form. Jesus said, "Unless you change and become like little children, you will never enter the kingdom of heaven" (Matt. 18:3 NIV). The manger scene helps children, and everyone who is childlike, visualize the baby and ponder why He was born—to become the perfect Man, the crucified King, and the risen Redeemer of the world.

How wonderful that Jesus did not suddenly appear on earth as a grown man in a UFO kind of descent to earth. God wanted us to see the picture—to be confident Jesus' incarnation was from the very departure of a womb. It was at a time and place. Numerous people witnessed it. It was recorded in history. We do not need a photo or video. God has recorded it in His Holy Book, and the pen of thousands of skilled poets have painted the scene. More importantly, He reveals Himself to us today through His Holy Spirit who opens our eyes and heart to know Him. Don't just look for the manger scene; look for the living Christ who went from the manger to be your Savior. Look at and accept His gift for you this Christmas.

Infant Holy, Infant Lowly

*You will find a baby wrapped in swaddling cloths
and lying in a manger. . . .
He is Lord of lords and King of kings.*

LUKE 2:12; REVELATION 17:14

W ZLOBIE LEZY
Text: Polish carol
Paraphrased, Edith M. G. Reed
Music: Traditional Polish melody

1. In - fant ho - ly, in - fant low - ly, for His bed a cat - tle stall;
2. Flocks were sleep-ing, shep-herds keep-ing vig - il till the morn-ing new

ox - en low - ing, lit - tle know-ing Christ, the babe, is Lord of all.
saw the glo - ry, heard the sto - ry, tid-ings of a gos-pel true.

Swift are wing-ing an-gels sing - ing, no - ëls ring - ing, tid-ings bring-ing:
Thus re - joic - ing, free from sor - row, prais - es voic - ing, greet the mor - row:

Christ the babe is Lord of all. Christ the babe is Lord of all.
Christ the babe was born for you. Christ the babe was born for you.

December 21   Lo, How a Rose E'er Blooming

TEXT: German Hymn, ca. 1500 ‖

First written in German around AD 1500, this beautiful poem was translated into English by three different people at three different times. This translation was created by Theodore Baker in 1894. The poem uses imagery from the prophet Isaiah to describe Jesus as the "Rose" and the "stem" of Jesse. Some translations of Isaiah use the words crocus or lily, but these flowers are both known as the roses of the desert. Jesus came like a rose to a dry, barren land.

He is also the stem of Jesse, descending from the line of Jesse, King David's father. The "men of old" in the song are the prophets, particularly Isaiah. The imagery continues: perhaps "cold of winter" refers to the Roman occupation and the 400 years of silence of the prophets. It was into this darkness for Israel that Jesus came. What might "when half-spent was the night" mean? Some think it means in the middle of the night, which is why many Christmas Eve services take place at midnight. It could also refer to the middle of human history as expressed by BC and AD, before and after Christ.

The first two stanzas tell a story with delightful flower metaphors. The final stanza explains the meaning of the imagery. The flower is Christ—"true man, yet very God."

TUNE: German Melody, 16th c. ‖

ES IST EIN' ROS' ENTSPRUNGEN is a German melody from the sixteenth century. Without knowing German, you might guess it means "a rose has sprung up." The prolific German organist, composer, and musicologist Michael Praetorius arranged the tune for congregational worship around 1602. The rhythm of the melody is not in a strict meter, so a quarter note is what you focus on in counting instead of a bar line.

As you sing this hymn . . . enjoy the beautiful and poetic ways that the birth of Jesus is portrayed. In this carol, you are provided a new lexicon of praise. The metaphors deserve our consideration:

Rose e're blooming	Christ is born
Sprung from tender stem	From the family tree
Amid the cold of winter	Coming when you might least expect
Flower of fragrance tender	Goodness of Jesus
Sweetness fills the air	Holy Spirit pervades
Dispels glorious splendor	Light of the World
Darkness everywhere	Sin ruling over the earth
Lightens every load	Righteousness brings peace

Read the prophecy of Isaiah 11:1 in "Christmas in the Bible," #3 that employs a nature metaphor in foretelling the lineage of Jesus; then Isaiah 35:1–2 says a rose will blossom in the desert. This carol is like a living Christmas card illustrating the contrasts from the natural order of life. Meditate in prayer on these metaphors.

Lo, How a Rose E'er Blooming 27

The wilderness and the solitary place shall be glad for them;
and the desert shall rejoice, and blossom as the rose.

ISAIAH 35:1–2 KJV

ES IST EIN' ROS' ENTSPRUNGEN
Text: German hymn, ca. 1500
Music: German melody, 16th c.

December 22   Away in a Manger

TEXT: Anonymous ‖

The author of "Away in a Manger" is uncertain. Most hymnologists believe that an American probably wrote at least the first two verses sometime in the middle of the nineteenth century. The Evangelical Lutheran Church was the first to publish this carol, beloved by children, in its *Little Children's Book: For School and Families* (1885). Two years later, hymn writer James R. Murray published it in *Dainty Songs for Little Lads and Lasses*. He must have heard the legend of Martin Luther's authorship since he titled it "Luther's Cradle Hymn," mistakenly claiming Luther had written it and sung it to his children every night. The third verse appeared in a collection called *Vineyard Songs* published in 1892 by Charles Gabriel.

TUNE: William James Kirkpatrick ‖ b. February 27, 1838, Duncannon, Pennsylvania
d. September 20, 1921, Germantown, Pennsylvania

There are two tunes commonly used for this carol: MUELLER and the less common CRADLE SONG, used more outside of America and included here. This tune is attributed to William Kirkpatrick but is almost identical to the Scottish folk song, "Flow Gently, Sweet Afton." Both tunes have the beauty and simplicity of folk songs and could be called lullabies. At least forty-one tunes have been used for this text.

As you sing this hymn . . . you may not be trying to lull a child to sleep, but the poem and melody do paint an idyllic picture of Jesus' birthplace. Possibly a barn or stable, it also may have been a lower level part of the home where animals could gather against cold. The Bible does not say "the cattle are lowing" or that Jesus was "asleep on the hay." But it does declare in Luke 2:7, 12, and 16 that He was in a manger. "Manger" comes from a Latin word that means "chew" or "eat" and is clearly a trough for animals. Surely Joseph or Mary would have cleaned it out as best they could and covered it with cloths including the swaddling cloths the angel described. But the angels' identifying sign for the shepherds to seek was a baby in a manger. How unlikely!

The manger was no accident. John Piper says:

> It becomes ludicrous to think that a God who wields an empire to move one woman from Nazareth to Bethlehem can't arrange for there to be an available guest room. Planning a bed for his Son was easier than planning a global census. Jesus was lying in exactly the place God planned: a feeding trough . . . The *Messiah* is in a feeding trough! Glory to God! The *Lord* is in a feeding trough! "Glory to God *in the highest!*" From the highest to the lowest! . . . The manger was step one on the Calvary road. The Calvary road is downhill. Not because it gets easier, but because it gets lower. The Savior's life starts low and ends lower, on a cross.[34]

Was baby Jesus' divine nature so perfectly contented that it is true, "no crying he makes"? Crying is a gift of communication from God so babies can let us know they need something. We know Jesus, the man, is recorded as weeping. We also know that we also can cry out, "be near me, Lord Jesus, I ask thee to stay . . . love me I pray." And He will.

Jesus . . . said to them, "Let the children come to me;
do not hinder them, for to such belongs the kingdom of God. . . ."
And he took them in his arms and blessed them,
laying his hands on them.

MARK 10:14, 16

CRADLE SONG
Text: Anonymous
Music: William J. Kirkpatrick

1. A - way in a____ man - ger, no____ crib for a bed,
2. The cat - tle are____ low - ing the____ Ba - by a - wakes,
3. Be near me, Lord____ Je - sus, I____ ask Thee to stay

the____ lit - tle Lord Je - sus lay____ down His sweet head;
but____ lit - tle Lord Je - sus, no____ cry - ing He makes;
close____ by me for - ev - er and____ love me I pray;

the stars in the____ bright sky looked down where He lay,
I love Thee, Lord____ Je - sus, look____ down from the sky,
bless all the dear____ child - ren in____ Thy ten - der care,

the____ lit - tle Lord Je - sus a - sleep on the hay.
and____ stay by my cra - dle 'til____ morn - ing is nigh.
and____ fit us for heav - en to____ live with Thee there.

TEXT: Joseph Mohr ‖ b. December 11, 1792, Salzburg, Austria
d. December 4, 1848, Wagrain, Austria

Joseph Mohr grew up in poverty, living with his mother and grandmother. His father, a soldier, was absent from his life. The choirmaster of his church saw potential in Joseph and served as his foster father. He saw to it that Joseph, an honor student, was well educated. Joseph went on to be ordained as a priest in 1815 and became a beloved pastor in several parishes throughout Austria. When he died, he was as poor as he had been as a child, having given away his money to educate the children and care for the elderly of his parish. Today, the Joseph Mohr School, a memorial from the townspeople, stands in the Alpine village of Wagrain, Austria, his last parish and burial place. Only a year after his ordination, Mohr wrote a poem while at his first parish at Mariapfarr, titled "Stille Nacht, Heilige Nacht." The Napoleonic wars had divided the country. A time of peace and calm was desperately needed.

TUNE: Franz Gruber ‖ b. November 25, 1787, Unterweizberg, Austria
d. June 7, 1863, Hallein, Austria

Two years later, Mohr was serving in Oberndorf where Franz Gruber was organist. Legend says that Mohr asked Gruber to write the tune for guitar because the church organ was broken. Although the broken organ theory has not been proven, the fact that it was a simple tune for guitar accompaniment is undisputed. It can be played with only three chords. It was first performed on December 24, 1818, for the midnight mass. STILLE NACHT is, of course, composed of the first two words of the song.

As you sing this hymn . . . do so quietly and calmly. Have you ever been present at the birth of a baby? It can be an atmosphere of hurry, nervousness, and even panic. But this carol paints a different picture of the birth of Jesus. The music portrays a calm, silent night. Why? Not because Mohr or Gruber knew that Jesus' birth was particularly peaceful, but because Jesus' birth alone would bring true peace to the world. The shepherds certainly had some excitement—"shepherds quake at the sight" and "they came with haste" (KJV). But we picture complete serenity and calm when they entered the stable.

Do you have difficulty finding silence and quiet? A friend tells of his annual hunting trip into the deep woods of upper Michigan. But he just purposes to sit perfectly still on a stump for long hours of quiet and simply watch the deer and the surrounding nature—an extended time to meditate and pray. Such silence is so absent in our lives in this noisy world.

Do you have a "silent night" in your Christmas? Do you see the "radiant beams from [His] holy face" because you have taken time to stop and look? Even in a noisy world, true peace and calm will come to those who know the baby Jesus as Lord and Savior. Psalm 131:2 gives us the picture: "I have calmed and quieted my soul, like a weaned child with its mother; like a weaned child is my soul within me." Because this carol is so closely associated with its German origin, the first stanza is given in German—a great reminder of the global love for the Christmas story.

Silent Night! Holy Night!

29

And they went with haste
and found Mary and Joseph,
and the baby lying in a manger.

LUKE 2:16

STILLE NACHT
Text: Joseph Mohr
Music: Franz Gruber

Stil - le Nacht! Hei - li - ge Nacht! Al - les schläft,
1. Si - lent night! Ho - ly night! All is calm,
2. Si - lent night! Ho - ly night! Shep - herds quake
3. Si - lent night! Ho - ly night! Son of God,
4. Si - lent night! Ho - ly night! Won - drous star,

ein - sam wacht nur das trau - te, hoch hei - li - ge Paar
all is bright 'round yon vir - gin moth - er and Child.
at the sight! Glo - ries stream from heav - en a - far,
love's pure light, ra - diant beams from Thy ho - ly face,
lend thy light; with the an - gels let us sing

hold - er Kna - be im lock - i - gen Harr, schlaf in himm - lisch-er
Ho - ly in - fant, so ten - der and mild, sleep in heav - en - ly
heav'n - ly hosts sing al - le - lu - ia; Christ, the Sav - ior, is
with the dawn of re - deem - ing grace, Je - sus, Lord, at Thy
al - le - lu - ia to our King; Christ, the Sav - ior, is

Ruh, schlaf in himm - lisch - er Ruh!
peace, sleep in heav - en - ly peace.
born! Christ, the Sav - ior, is born!
birth, Je - sus, Lord, at Thy birth.
born! Christ, the Sav - ior, is born!

December 24   O Holy Night

TEXT: Placide Cappeau	b. October 25, 1808, Roquemaure, France
Translated, John S. Dwight	d. August 8, 1877, Roquemarure, France
	b. May 13, 1813, Boston, Massachusetts
	d. September 5, 1893, Boston, Massachusetts

For a Christmas Eve service in 1847, Placide Cappeau was asked by a parish priest in his town to write a Christmas poem. It is believed he actually wrote it while traveling in a stagecoach. Although Cappeau, a socialist, had little belief in the Christmas story, he realized upon completing the poem that there was something special about it. He asked a musician friend, Adophe Adams, to write a melody. In 1855, American journalist and Unitarian minister John Dwight heard the song and created an English edition. Though his translation is very singable, a literal translation of the French is even more clearly and pointedly an expression of the gospel.

TUNE: Adophe C. Adams	b. July 24, 1803, Paris, France,
	d. May 3, 1856, Paris, France

A professional composer, Adophe Adams was famous at the time for his composition of numerous operas and ballets. Because Adams was of Jewish heritage, accepting the commission to write the tune for Cappeau's poem was for Adams no more than a professional endeavor. However, this is the music for which he is best known. After a Handel aria, it was the second song ever broadcast on early radio, Christmas Eve, 1906. Capturing the drama of opera, it has been sung and recorded by more famous singers and choirs than perhaps any other Christmas carol. Yet because of its familiarity, it is also singable by most people.

As you sing this hymn . . . you are experiencing a perfect example of how God uses all things and people to accomplish His purpose and display His glory. Written by a man with little belief in the Christmas story, put to music by a nonbelieving Jewish musician, and translated by a liberal theologian, this carol proclaims the truth in a compelling song for the ages. Because of these origins, however, it was banned by the French Catholic church as being unfit. But the French people continued to sing it, and soon the song spread around the world. It brought conviction to slave owners worldwide. On Christmas Eve, it was sung across French and German battle lines during WWI. How amazing to see the hand of God in its creation as well as its use by believers and nonbelievers alike.

There is a definite progression in the song. The first stanza identifies the *need*, "Long lay the world in sin and error pining." Christ appeared and "the weary world rejoices." The second verse tells us of the *heart* of Christ for this world: "In all our trials, born to be our friend. He knows our needs, to our weakness is no stranger." In the final stanza, we are given guidance for how we should live: "He taught us to love one another . . . the slave is our brother." Finally, we are entreated in the ultimate response we all must make to this encounter with the babe of Bethlehem: "Fall on your knees . . . Christ is the Lord, O to praise His name forever . . . His power and glory evermore proclaim." Hardly a clearer or more important sermon could we hear on Christmas Eve.

O Holy Night

30

As I live, says the Lord,
every knee shall bow to me;
and every tongue shall confess to God.

ROMANS 14:11

CANTIQUE DE NOEL
Text: John S. Dwight
Music: Adolphe Adam

1. O ho-ly night,_ the stars are bright-ly shin - ing, it is the
2. Led by the light_ of faith se-ren-ly beam - ing, with glow-ing
3. Tru - ly He taught us to love_ one an - oth - er; His law is

night of the dear Sav-ior's birth; long lay the world_ in sin and er - ror
hearts by His cra-dle we stand; so led by light of a star_ sweet-ly
love, and His gos-pel is peace; chains shall He break for the slave_ is our

pin-ing, till He ap-peared and the soul_ felt its worth. A thrill of hope the
gleam-ing, here came the wise men_ from the O-rient land. The King of kings lay
broth - er, and in His name all op-pres-sion shall cease. Sweet hymns of joy in

wea-ry world re-joic - es, for yon-der breaks a new and glo-rious morn!
thus in low-ly man-ger, in all our tri - als born to be our friend!
grate-ful cho-rus raise we; let all with-in us praise His ho - ly name!

Fall_ on your knees!_ O hear_ the an-gel voic - es! O night_ di-
He_ knows our need,_ to our weak - ness is no strang-er. Be-hold_ your
Christ is the Lord!_ O praise_ His name for-ev - er! His pow'r_ and

vine!_ O_ night_ when Christ was born! O night_ di-
King!_ Be - fore_ Him low-ly bend!_ Be - hold_ your
glo - ry_ ev - er more pro-claim! His pow'r_ and

1.2. vine!_ O night, O night di-vine!
King:_ be - fore Him low-ly bend!
3. glo - ry_ ev - er more_ pro-claim!

December 25 O Come, All Ye Faithful

TEXT AND TUNE: John Francis Wade ‖ b. Circa 1710[35]
d. August 16, 1786, Douai, France

Englishman John Francis Wade was a Catholic layman at a time when persecution drove many Catholics to flee England for France. To support himself in his new country, Wade became a music copyist, known for his exquisitely beautiful handwritten copies of plainsongs and sacred music. In the process, he discovered a Latin poem that began "*Adeste Fidelis, Laeti triumphantes.*" From that, he composed the carol we know as "O Come, All Ye Faithful." Formerly, it was believed that he merely found and translated the carol, but more recently, musicologists determined that he indeed wrote the Latin carol text.

The carol was translated from the Latin into English almost one hundred years later by Reverend Frederick Oakley for his congregation at the Margaret Street Chapel in London. His first attempt was "Ye Faithful, Approach Ye." Several years later, and after he had converted to Catholicism increasing his skill in Latin, he tried again, writing the English words we know and which are now translated into over 150 languages.

ADESTE FIDELES (*Adeste*, "come"; *Fideles*, "faithful ones") was written by Wade for his own text and is named for the first two words. It first appeared in 1751 in his *Cantus Diversi*, music compiled for use in the Roman Catholic Church. Almost one hundred years later in 1845, Samuel Webbe, organist at the Portuguese embassy in London, arranged it in its present form. It is therefore sometimes called PORTUGUESE HYMN. It is also the tune used in Great Britain for the text "How Firm a Foundation."

As you sing this hymn . . . if you are following our calendar, it is Christmas Day. We sing in the present tense of Jesus, "born this happy morning, now in flesh appearing." And you are being called to worship—called with all the "faithful" to come on this Christmas Day and adore Him. The faithful are those who believe and affirm what this carol declares. The second stanza reflects the Nicene Creed, a profession of faith established by a council of church leaders at Nicaea, Turkey, in AD 325. As you sing, you are declaring, "This is what I believe." I believe He was true God and eternally existed, but began life on earth as planted by God in the womb of Virgin Mary. He was Son of the eternal Father, begotten and not created. These essential truths are beyond our comprehension but fundamental to our accepting the redemption plan of God.

Within the refrain's threefold invitation to "adore Him," we understand the essence of worship is not physical actions or outward homage, but it must be "in spirit and in truth." We adore what we most highly value. He must be, in the words of Sheldon Vanauken, "overwhelmingly *first*."[36] We adore whatever we place first in our lives, and God is worthy to be first. With all the distractions of Christmas, it is easy to sing about adoration without actually doing it. Take time today to quietly adore and once again express your faithfulness. Join the choirs of angels who sing, "Glory to God in the highest," and in so doing, make this your highest Christmas gift to Jesus.

O Come, All Ye Faithful

31

*Let us go over to Bethlehem
and see this thing that has happened,
which the Lord has made known to us.*

LUKE 2:15

ADESTE FIDELES
Text: Latin Hymn, Attr. to John Francis Wade
Music: John Francis Wade's *Cantus Diversi*, 1751

A - des - te, fi - de - les, læ - ti tri - um - phan - tes;
1. O come, all ye faith - ful, joy - ful and tri - um - phant,
2. God of God, Light of Light;
3. Sing, choirs of an - gels, sing in ex - ul - ta - tion,
4. Yea, Lord, we greet Thee, born this hap - py morn - ing:

Ve - ni - te, ve - ni - te in Beth - le - hem.
O come ye, O come ye to Beth - le - hem;
lo, He ab - hors not the Vir - gin's womb:
sing, all ye cit - i - zens of heav'n a - bove;
Je - sus, to Thee be all glo - ry giv'n;

Na - tum vi - de - te, Re - gem an - ge - lo - rum.
come and be - hold Him born the King of an - gels;
ver - y God, be - got - ten, not cre - a - ted;
glo - ry to God, glo - ry in the high - est;
Word of the Fa - ther, now in flesh ap - pear - ing;

Ve - ni - te a - do - re - mus, ve - ni - te a - do - re - mus,
O come, let us a - dore Him, O come, let us a - dore Him,

Ve - ni - te - a - do - re - mus Do - mi - num.
O come, let us a - dore Him, Christ the Lord.

83

EPIPHANY

AFTER CHRISTMAS, the church calendar enters twelve days of Epiphany. These conclude on January 6. A dictionary defines an epiphany as a sudden manifestation or perception of the nature of something, *or* an illuminating discovery, realization, or disclosure. To have an epiphany is to say, "Aha!" or "Oh, I get it!" or "Now the light dawns!" That is what we should experience on the other side of Christmas.

Christmas Day is typically a school and work holiday, as well as a day for exchanging gifts. People then assume it concludes at midnight of December 25. Soon we put away the decorations and return to our routines of life. Except for a lighthearted song about the "Twelve Days of Christmas," few know there is more to celebrate. Never mind the 1,500-year-old church tradition of continuing the season for twelve days. Perhaps we should leave our decorations up for several days into the New Year to help remind us of Christ's birth.

During Epiphany, we consider the coming of the wise men to see Jesus, even though they probably visited the child months or even years after Jesus was born. Yet the visit of these non-Israelites reveals that Jesus was born for the Gentiles as well as the Jews. He is Messiah for the entire world.

Just as the star illumined the path of the wise men, so God sheds light into our hearts to guide us to Him. Just as the wise men stood in awe and wonder so that they "fell down and worshiped Him," we too should consider the coming of Christ in awe and wonder. We too should bow in humble submission to this One whose birth we have celebrated.

Like the wise men, we bring our best to God in Christ, at least in one sense. In another, perhaps more important sense, we bring our worst— our sin, our guilt, our brokenness. As the eighteenth-century hymn writer Joseph Hart put it:

> *Come, ye weary, heavy-laden,*
> *Lost and ruined by the fall;*
> *If you tarry 'til you're better,*
> *You will never come at all.*
>
> .   .   .   .
>
> *Lo! th' incarnate God ascended,*
> *Pleads the merit of His blood:*
> *Venture on Him, venture wholly,*
> *Let no other trust intrude.*
>
> *I will arise and go to Jesus,*
> *He will embrace me in His arms;*
> *In the arms of my dear Savior,*
> *Oh, there are ten thousand charms.*[37]

So forget about the two turtledoves or the partridge in a pear tree. Instead, spend the twelve days after Christmas arising and going to this Jesus. Don't think on the "charms" you can bring. Expect instead the ten thousand charms and embrace and life eternal He has for you.

THIS IS THE MONTH, AND THIS THE HAPPY MORN
Wherein the son of heaven's eternal king,
Of wedded maid and virgin mother born,
Our great redemption from above did bring;
For so the holy sages once did sing,
That he our deadly forfeit should release,
And with his father work us a perpetual peace.

That glorious form, that light insufferable,
And that far-beaming blaze of majesty,
Wherewith he wont at heaven's high council-table,
To sit the midst of trinal unity,
He laid aside; and here with us to be,
Forsook the courts of everlasting day,
And chose with us a darksome house of mortal clay.

Say heavenly muse, shall not thy sacred vein
Afford a present to the infant God?
Hast thou no verse, no hymn, or solemn strain,
To welcome him to this his new abode,
Now while the heaven by the sun's team untrod,
Hath took no print of the approaching light,
And all the spangled host keep watch in squadrons bright?

See how from far upon the eastern road
The star-led wizards haste with odors sweet!
O run, prevent them with thy humble ode,
And lay it lowly at his blessed feet;
Have thou the honor first, thy Lord to greet,
And join thy voice unto the angel choir,
From out his secret altar touched with hallowed fire.

. . . . . .

Such music (as 'tis said)
Before was never made,
But when of old the sons of morning sung;
While the creator great
His constellations set,
And the well-balanced world on hinges hung,
And cast the dark foundations deep,
And bid the weltering waves their oozy channel keep.

Ring out ye crystal spheres,
Once bless our human ears,
(If ye have power to touch our senses so)
And let your silver chime
Move in melodious time;
And let the base of heaven's deep organ blow;
And with your ninefold harmony
Make up full consort to the angelic symphony

JOHN MILTON, 1608–1674[38]

December 26 Joy to the World! The Lord Is Come

TEXT: Isaac Watts ‖ b. July 17, 1674, Southampton, England
d. November 25, 1748, Stoke Newington, England

Isaac Watt's father was a leader in the Nonconformist State Church movement, and he was repeatedly imprisoned for his views. Watts was an exceptionally bright child, learning Latin by age four, Greek at age nine, French at eleven, and Hebrew at age thirteen. Though offered free education at Oxford or Cambridge, he refused and attended the Nonconformist Academy. In 1702, Watts became pastor of London's Mark Lane Independent Church. Although he wrote many volumes of books on theology, and there remain many books of his sermons, it is by his hymns that Watts is known today.

Watts was never satisfied with the congregational singing in churches. In his later years, he wrote, "To see the dull indifference, the negligent and thoughtless air that sits upon the faces of a whole assembly, while the psalm is upon their lips, might even tempt a charitable observer to suspect the fervency of their inward religion."[39] To counter this, he determined to write hymns that elicited joy and natural fervency, with "Joy to the World" a primary example and probably one of the most recognized and commonly sung Christmas carols in the world.

TUNE: Lowell Mason ‖ b. January 8, 1792, Medfield, Massachusetts
d. August 11, 1872, Orange, New Jersey

Lowell Mason was largely responsible for introducing music into American public schools and is considered to be the first significant music educator in the United States. But he was also a leading figure in American church music, writing over 1,600 hymns. Like Watts, Mason sought better congregational singing. At his church, Fifth Avenue Presbyterian in New York City, he fired all of the hired musicians except the organist, and his church became known for having the most excellent congregational singing in the city.

Mason attributed the tune ANTIOCH to G. F. Handel and several parts of the melody can be found throughout *Messiah*. ANTIOCH is the name of the city in Syria mentioned in Acts 11:26 where believers were first called Christians.

As you sing this hymn . . . you are singing a Christmas hymn that never mentions Christmas. Based on Psalm 98:4–9, there is no baby in a manger, no angels, no shepherds or wise men, only that He "is come." Present tense! He reigns and rules with truth and grace, both now and in the future. Please turn to "Christmas in the Bible," #40. This is a continuing Advent, Christmas, and Epiphany event, a song that can be sung year-round.

What is it about this song that has captured our hearts and made it is so central to Christmas music? Marshall Segal of Desiring God Ministries says of this carol: "The story of the world meeting Jesus in the flesh is a story of the world finally finding full joy in God."[40] We live in essentially a joyless world. Everyone longs for joy. We might wonder, what do nonbelievers think when they are singing this carol? From what lasting place is their joy if they do not believe in this reigning King? Even fields, floods, rocks, hills, and plains rejoice, so Christians surely can be joyful! He rules over sin and sorrow, over thorns in our lives, and puts a stop to the curse of death that all are under. "Let every heart prepare Him room," and pure joy will come to you. Sing for joy at the "wonders of His love."

Joy to the World! The Lord Is Come

32

Make a joyful noise unto the LORD, all the earth:
make a loud noise, and rejoice,
and sing praise.

PSALM 98:4 KJV

ANTIOCH
Text: Isaac Watts
Music: Lowell Mason

December 27   Joy Has Dawned upon the World

TEXT: Stuart Townend ‖ b. June 1, 1963, West Yorkshire, England

Stuart Townend was a literature major at the University of Sussex in Brighton, England. His texts reflect this scholarship and are spiritually deep and filled with Scripture. He states,

> Songs don't just have to give us an "experience." They can teach us and challenge us. They can retell the stories of the Bible in a meaningful way. They can also (like the Psalms) attempt to explore the joys and sorrows of the human condition in the light of our faith. These kinds of songs may not "push the happy button" for a congregation, but nonetheless they are vital in grounding our faith in reality.[41]

Townend and Keith Getty wrote this song while working on a larger project titled "Creed," referring to the Apostle's Creed. They had realized there is a shortage of newer hymns on important Christian foundations such as the incarnation, God coming into our world through Jesus as a human being.

TUNE: Keith Getty ‖ b. December 16, 1974, Lisburn, North Ireland

Keith Getty characterizes this hymn as a Christmas version of "In Christ Alone." It tells the story of Christmas, from prophecy to wise men, just as "In Christ Alone" tells the whole gospel story. When performing this hymn in concert, Getty and his wife, Kristyn, often pair it with the refrain "Gloria in excelsis Deo" of "Angels We Have Heard on High."

As you sing this hymn . . . think about the beautiful experience of dawn! Nighttime darkness, terrors, and fear are all shattered at that very first ray of light. Every twenty-four hours, dawn is a reminder that in the dark, oppressive world of the first century BC, one tiny wail in a dark and lonely manger forever crushed sin and the dominion of darkness. Did everyone know and see it then? No, but we can now look back and wonder at the unfolding mystery of God since creation. The light has dawned, and it continues to dawn upon people in whom God's Spirit reveals Himself.

But we live in an age when we expect the spectacular. We would like the declarations of God and His plan for us to be written across the sky. We are used to Hollywood productions, even in Christian media. In a long out-of-print Christian satirical periodical called *The Wittenberg Door*, we remember a cartoon picturing a church production with big orchestra, multiple choirs, flashing colored lights, set, drama, and animals. Under it, the caption read, "First Church presents the simple story of Christmas."

How ironic that "not with fanfare or scenes of glory" but with the simple birth of a baby, God communicated that He loves us. This carol could be sung year-round as it declares what God was doing—paying a ransom, reconciling, becoming champion over sin and death, and becoming our Savior and even our Friend! There have been great men, great leaders, and great rulers in history, but here we declare that Jesus is the "Lord of history"! The simplicity of the story may puzzle you, the humility of God in Christ will astound you, but the truth of what Jesus came to earth to do should change you forever.

Joy Has Dawned upon the World

33

We also have the prophetic message as something completely reliable,
and you will do well to pay attention to it, as to a light shining in a dark place,
until the day dawns and the morning star rises in your hearts.

2 PETER 1:19 NIV

Text and Music:
Stuart Townend, Keith Getty

1. Joy has dawned up - on the world, pro - mised from cre - a - tion: God's sal - va - tion now un - furled, hope for e - v'ry na - tion. Not with fan - fares from a - bove, not with scenes of glo - ry, but a hum - ble gift of love, Je - sus born of Ma - ry.

2. Sounds of won - der fill the sky with the songs of an - gels, as the migh - ty Prince of Life shel - ters in a sta - ble. Hands that set each star in place, shaped the earth in dark - ness, cling now to a moth - er's breast, vul - ne - ra - ble and help - less.

3. Shep - herds bow be - fore the Lamb, gaz - ing at the glo - ry; Gifts of men from dis - tant lands proph - e - sy the sto - ry. Gold, a King is born to - day, in - cense, God is with us, myrrh, His death will make a way, and by blood He'll win us.

4. Son of A - dam, Son of heav'n, giv - en as a ran - som; re - con - cil - ing God and man, Christ our migh - ty Champ - ion! What a Sav - ior! What a Friend! What a glo - rious myst - 'ry: Once a babe in Beth - le - hem, now the Lord of hist - 'ry.

December 28   Go, Tell It on the Mountain

TEXT: John Wesley Work Jr. ‖ b. August 6, 1872, Nashville, Tennessee
d. September 7, 1925, Nashville, Tennessee

The spirituals from enslaved African Americans are a rich contribution to hymnody. Often these songs were created in the fields as they worked and then passed on from generation to generation. Many were preserved through the effort of John Wesley Work and his two sons, John Jr. and Frederick, together with the Jubilee Singers of Fisk University. After the Civil War, John Sr. was an African American church choir director in Nashville, Tennessee. His sons carried on his passion to preserve this music, finding many original tunes in the Appalachian Mountains and valleys. John Jr. is credited with finding and writing the spiritual "Go, Tell It on the Mountain."

TUNE: Spiritual ‖

The creators improvised on their tunes (as with the texts). Most are simple and follow the pentatonic (five note) scale. This is what you hear if you play only the five black keys on the piano. The song can be sung as a round without producing dissonance. The rhythm of this tune is strong and energetic, using a jazz shuffle. This pattern uses dotted eighth notes connected to sixteenth notes rather than successive, even eighth notes. The tune is named for its first words, GO TELL IT.

The Jubilee Singers introduced the entire nation and the world to this music. They sang before Queen Victoria and President Chester Arthur. The famous composer Antonín Dvořák said of this music, "In the Negro melodies of America I discover all that is needed for a great and noble school of music. . . . They are pathetic (moving, heart-rending), tender, passionate, melancholy, solemn, religious, bold, merry, gay. It is music that suits itself to any mood or purpose."[42]

As you sing this hymn . . . you are doing what every family does after a new baby is born: they go tell all their family and friends! Joy that is kept to yourself is incomplete. Sharing it completes the joy. If you see a beautiful sunset you want to say to those around you, "Look at that!" The shepherds could not keep it to themselves as they left the manger. Read again the Luke account as found in "Christmas in the Bible," #24–26. They spread the word concerning what they had seen and heard, and all who heard it were amazed.

This carol is the believer's call to tell people the real meaning of Christmas. It is the call of every Christian to share the joy so that all may come and find freedom from the slavery that sin has over them. Some people are slaves to sin without even realizing it. They think they have freedom to do as they please; but in truth, they are bound by the power of darkness. Jesus went to a mountain where He told people the good news. In the Sermon on the Mount, He said, "A city on a hill cannot be hidden . . . in the same way, let your light shine before others, that they may see your good works and give glory to your Father who is in heaven" (Matt. 5:14, 16).

How soon the good feelings and love we share at Christmas are abandoned and we return to business as usual. But God wants us to carry the message and even the spirit of Christmas throughout the entire year. Remember, "Good News" begins with the letters GO.

Go, Tell It on the Mountain

34

When they had seen him, they spread the word concerning
what had been told them about this child.

LUKE 2:17 NIV

Text: John W. Work Jr.
Music: Spiritual

Go, tell it on the moun - tain, o - ver the hills and ev - 'ry - where;

go, tell it on the moun - tain that Je - sus Christ is born. *Fine*

1. While shep - herds kept their watch-ing o'er si - lent flocks by night,
2. The shep - herds feared and trem - bled when, lo! a - bove the earth
3. Down in a low - ly man - ger our hum - ble Christ was born,

be - hold, through-out the heav-ens there shone a ho - ly light.____
rang out the an - gel cho - rus that hailed our Sav - ior's birth.____
and God sent us sal - va - tion that bless - ed Christ-mas morn.____ *D.C.*

TEXT AND TUNE: Traditional English Carol ‖ First appeared in print, 1823
Carols Ancient and Modern, William Sandys

The origin of this much-loved carol is unknown and is likely a genuine folk song as opposed to a hymn composed for the church. Though the English are credited with its origin, the word "noel" comes from the French expression "joyeux noël," which means Merry Christmas! In England, the word is spelled "nowell." Used in the context of the first phrase, the meaning may be from the root of the French word "nouvelles," which means "news." There are several indications that the original was by someone with minimal education as the grammar is forced in order to rhyme ("Our blest Messiah's place it was"). Even more, they may have had a minimal biblical education (as copies of the Bible were not readily available), for the second stanza mention of a star seen by the shepherds is nowhere in the biblical account. The writer might not have considered that it could have been spring or even known that a "cold winter's night" in Palestine was nothing like winter in England or France.

In spite of these things, the carol abounds with joy in its simple narrative of the Christmas story. Although most hymnals only provide four or five stanzas, up to nine can be found in older books. Unusual for English folk melodies, it is one musical phrase sung twice with a refrain of minimal variation and ending on the third note of the scale. The four-part hymn arrangement was created in 1871 by the famous English composer, John Stainer.

As you sing this hymn . . . because of the familiarity of the story, it is easy to overlook the wonder. Shepherds, the lowest, and wise men, the highest echelon of society, represent both extremes of our world as they encounter the baby Jesus. Were the wise men disappointed when, after such a long journey and an amazing celestial miracle, they were led to the poorest of locations and the birth to an unknown family? No. Their response, like the shepherds, is kneeling in adoration. There is no sense of confusion or wondering if they made a mistake. They simply worshiped. They trusted the word from God to avoid King Herod in their return home. Their lives were changed by this baby King.

What about yours? Are you pursuing Jesus and His light? If you are and you submit to Him, your life will never be the same. Just as the angels told the shepherds: "Fear not!" This King was born, not to enslave you, but to free you. His life, death, and resurrection will bring you eternal life if you "follow the star."

An excellent way to sing this carol is to have different family members sing the stanzas and everyone join on the refrain. Creative families might even make up their own stanzas to tell the story another way. It's all good news!

The First Noel

35

*The star that they had seen when it rose went before them
until it came to rest over the place where the child was.
When they saw the star, they rejoiced exceedingly
with great joy.*

MATTHEW 2:9–10

Text: English Carol, 17th c.
Music: English melody, Arr. John Stainer

December 30   As with Gladness Men of Old

TEXT: William Chatterton Dix || b. June 14, 1837, Bristol, England
d. September 9, 1898, Cheddar, Somerset, England

Willam Dix lived in England during the nineteenth century when romantic poetry was at its height. His father, a surgeon, loved poetry, especially that of Thomas Chatterton. He passed on to his son both the poet's name and his love of poetry. Although insurance was his business, William's passion was poetry, particularly as it was used in worship. He wrote over forty hymns and poems. It was said of him, "Few modern writers have shown so single a gift as his for the difficult art of hymn-writing."[43]

In his twenties, Dix acquired a serious and mysterious illness that kept him in bed for months. He became severely depressed, but it was during this time that he explored the Scriptures and wrote many of his hymns. On Epiphany Day, January 6, 1865, as Dix reflected upon the Scripture he would have read at church had he not been ill (Matt. 2:1– 12), he began to write a poem. He titled it "The Manger Throne," which later became "As with Gladness Men of Old." "What Child Is This?" is another carol derived from the same poem. Dix refers to the "men of old" in the story rather than "kings" or "magi" because so much of the information about them comes from tradition and myth rather than the testimony of the Scripture.

TUNE: Conrad Kocher || b. December 16, 1786, Württemberg, Germany
d. March 12, 1872, Stuttgart, Germany

The tune carries the name of the author, DIX, but it was first written by a German composer, Conrad Kocher. An Englishman named William Henry Monk adapted it for this carol. We also sing "For the Beauty of the Earth" to the same melody.

As you sing this hymn . . . imagine these serious strangers from the East expressing such gladness and joy at their discovery. Matthew describes it as "exceeding great joy." The wise men had studied astronomy and saw the star that God had used to mark the place where Jesus was born. They traveled for months, possibly years, to find Him. Perhaps they had staked reputations and fortune on this venture. God rewarded their faith and used it to announce something profound. Just as these men were foreigners to ancient Israel, so were the Gentiles. Up to this point in history, the Messiah was for the nation of Israel, God's people. The lesson of Epiphany is that God's Son and salvation through Him are for the entire world, not just the Jews. The wise men were the first Gentiles to understand this gift to all.

Dix's father told his son that he liked the way in which the conclusion of each stanza tells the singer how to respond to the birth of Jesus. Too often the carols simply leave us with a beautiful picture. As you sing, you are asking God to help you be like those early seekers, seeking, kneeling, offering gifts, praising for all eternity your heavenly King.

As with Gladness Men of Old 36

*When they saw the star, they rejoiced exceedingly
with great joy. . . . they fell down and worshiped him.
Then, opening their treasures, they offered him gifts.*

MATTHEW 2:10–11

DIX
Text: William Chatterton Dix
Music: Conrad Kocher

1. As with gladness men of old did the guid-ing star be-hold;
2. As with joy-ful steps they sped to that low-ly man-ger bed,
3. As they of-fered gifts most rare at that man-ger rude and bare,
4. Ho-ly Je-sus, ev-ery day keep us in the nar-row way;

as with joy they hailed its light, lead-ing on-ward, beam-ing bright,
there to bend the knee be-fore Him Whom heaven and earth a-dore,
so may we with ho-ly joy, pure and free from sin's al-loy,
and when earth-ly things are past, bring our ran-somed souls at last

so, most gra-cious Lord, may we ev-er-more be led to Thee.
so, may we with will-ing feet ev-er seek Thy mer-cy seat.
all our cost-liest trea-sures bring, Christ, to Thee, our heav'n-ly King.
where they need no star to guide, where no clouds Thy glo-ry hide.

December 31   Standing at the Portal

TEXT AND TUNE: Frances R. Havergal ‖ b. December 14, 1836, Astley, Worcestershire, England
d. June 3, 1879, Swansea, Wales

Frances, or Fanny, Havergal was the youngest daughter of her family, raised during Britain's Victorian period. Her father was a pastor and hymn writer. As a precocious child, she was nicknamed "Little Quicksilver" by her father. Even at a young age, she could quote from the Psalms, Isaiah, the Minor Prophets, and the New Testament. At age fifteen, Havergal wrote, "I committed my soul to the Savior, and earth and heaven seemed brighter from that moment."[44] She attended college in Germany where she learned several modern languages, including Greek and Hebrew. She loved writing poems and music and developed into a talented singer and pianist.

When Havergal was eleven, she lost her mother to illness and was never healthy herself. When her doctor ultimately told her that she would not live much longer, because of her strong faith she replied, "That is too good to be true." Because her life ended at only forty-two, she has been called "a bright but short-lived candle in English hymnody." Over fifty of her hymns were published in various hymnals, but two of her most widely sung and loved hymns are "Take My Life, and Let It Be" and "Like a River Glorious." In her own words, her primary goal was to be a "personal spiritual benefit upon others."[45]

Her hymn tune, HERMAS, was written in 1871 when she was thirty-five. It is more well-known as the tune for the hymn "On Our Way Rejoicing." The tune ST. ALBAN is associated as well with "Standing at the Portal." It was written by Franz Joseph Haydn, and adds a four-phrase refrain: "Onward then, and fear not, children of the day; for His Word shall never, never pass away."

As you sing this hymn . . . you are obviously not singing a Christmas hymn, but instead one to be sung (or recited if you do not know the tune) on New Year's Eve. The custom of the New Year's Eve "Watchnight Services" is seldom practiced in churches today. There are few hymns written and almost none placed in modern hymnals that even mention this unique evening. Perhaps sadly any gatherings on that evening are given to parties and feasting. However, praying in the new year was the purpose of the traditional New Year's Eve service and could still be a family's practice, whether at the midnight hour or earlier in the evening. Prayers based on Scripture promises should be made, and this hymn provides a solid foundation for those prayers.

Jim Elliot, a missionary martyred for his faith, wrote regarding the new year: "I pray that the Lord might crown this year with His goodness and in the coming one give you a hallowed dare-devil spirit in lifting the biting sword of Truth, consuming you with a passion that is called by the cultured citizen of Christendom 'fanaticism,' but known to God as that saintly madness that led His Son through bloody sweat and hot tears to agony on a rude Cross . . . and Glory!"[46]

That is a resolution! Our customary New Year's resolutions of losing weight or changing a habit pale in comparison. God wants our continuing resolves to trust His faithfulness and love, not only on New Year's Day but throughout the year. Jonathan Edwards wrote this resolution: "Resolution One: I will live for God. Resolution Two: If no one else does, I will."[47] As you "stand at the portal," what is your resolve for the coming year?

Standing at the Portal

It is the LORD who goes before you.
He will be with you; he will not leave you or forsake you.
Do not fear or be dismayed.

DEUTERONOMY 31:8

HERMAS
Text: Frances R. Havergal
Music: Frances R. Havergal

1. Stand - ing at the por - tal of the o - pening year,
words of com - fort meet us, hush - ing ev - er - y fear;
spo - ken through the si - lence by our Fa - ther's voice,
ten - der, strong, and faith - ful, mak - ing us re - joice.

2. "I the LORD am with you. Do not be a - fraid,
I will help and strength - en; do not be dis - mayed!
For I will up - hold you with My own right hand;
You are called and cho - sen in My sight to stand."

3. For the year be - fore us, O what rich sup - plies,
For the poor and need - y liv - ing streams shall rise;
For the sad and sin - ful shall His grace a - bound;
For the faint and fee - ble per - fect strength be found.

4. He will nev - er fail us, He will not for - sake;
His e - ter - nal cov - 'nant He will nev - er break.
Rest - ing on His prom - ise, what have we to fear?
God is all - suf - fi - cient for the com - ing year.

January 1   O Rejoice, Ye Christians, Loudly

TEXT: Christian Keimann

Translated, Catherine Winkworth

b. February 27, 1607, Pankratz, Habsburg, Bohemia

d. January 1662, Zittau, Germany

After studies at the University of Wittenberg, Christian Keimann became a Lutheran pastor. In the German city of Zittau, near the Czech and Polish borders, he was initially the associate director of an elite school but became its rector in 1638. There, Keimann became prolific at the writing of hymns. A strong tradition in Zittau was to celebrate each Christmas with a town festival and pageant telling the nativity story. He wrote the play and this hymn text to be used in the performance, collaborating with Andreas Hammerschmidt who wrote the music.

TUNE: Andreas Hammerschmidt

b. December 1611, Brüx, Bohemia, Germany

d. October 29, 1675, Zittau, Germany

Andreas Hammerschmidt was a German Bohemian composer and organist, known as the "Orpheus of Zittau." He was one of the most significant and famous composers of sacred music in Germany in the mid-seventeenth century. On August 22, 1637, he married Ursula Teuffel, the daughter of a Prague businessman, and they had six children. Hammerschmidt wrote motets, concertos, and arias, but most of his output is sacred vocal music in the concertato style. This form has melodies offered between opposing groups of voices or groups of musicians. His church contained three organs opposite each other and thus provided ideal possibilities for writing and performing this concerted style. The great J. S. Bach used the first stanza of this hymn (chorale) in one of his cantatas, and the harmonization in the accompaniment to this hymn is from Bach.

As you sing this hymn . . . it is critical to remember that the years of Keimann's and Hammerschmidt's lives coincide almost entirely with the Thirty Years War in Central Europe (1618–1648). One of the longest and most destructive conflicts, many consider it to be the worst European religious war in history, with over eight million deaths. Over the years, it devastated entire regions, with famine and disease resulting in high mortality in the populations of the German and Italian states and even the Netherlands. Both armies traditionally looted or extorted tribute to get operating funds, which imposed severe hardships on the inhabitants of occupied territories.

Through all of this, God's devoted people proclaimed faith and continued to celebrate the birth of Christ. The refrain mentions sadness, but "done away with." It mentions "sorrow and repining," but proclaims the "Son of grace shines" over them. The people's anticipation of the new year as mentioned in stanza four is not filled with dread or fear but with gladness. The hymn implores worshipers to consider the wondrous thing God has done through His incarnation and that He chooses to live with us. Though beginning in a minor key, the tune gradually transposes and ends with a strong major chord. This refrain virtually sparkles with joy as it builds. Bach's bass harmony winds up like a catapult to proclaim the final exclamation, defying the stereotypes of troubles, much less war. May its truth defy any sadness, hardship, or grief in your life as you meditate on and sing the declarations of each phrase, making it your triumphal song for the New Year.

O Rejoice, Ye Christians, Loudly 38

And the ransomed of the LORD shall return
and come to Zion with singing;
everlasting joy shall be upon their heads;
they shall obtain gladness and joy, and sorrow and sighing shall flee away.

ISAIAH 35:10

FREUET EUCH, IHR CHRISTEN ALLE
Text: Christian Keimann, Tr. Catherine Winkworth
Music: Andreas Hammerschmidt

1. O re-joice, ye Chris-tians, loud-ly, for our joy has now be-gun;
2. See, my soul, your Sav-ior choos-es weak-ness here and pov-er-ty;
3. Lord, how shall I thank Thee right-ly? I ac-knowl-edge that by Thee
4. Je-sus, guard and guide Thy mem-bers; fill them with Thy bound-less grace;

won-drous things our God has done. Tell a-broad His good-ness proud-ly;
in such love He comes to thee. Nei-ther crib nor cross re-fus-ing,
I am saved e-ter-nal-ly. Let me not for-get it light-ly
hear their prayers in ev-ery place. Fan to flame faith's glow-ing em-bers;

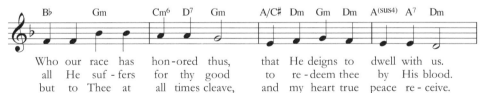

Who our race has hon-ored thus, that He deigns to dwell with us.
all He suf-fers for thy good to re-deem thee by His blood.
but to Thee at all times cleave, and my heart true peace re-ceive.
grant all Chris-tians, far and near, ho-ly peace, a glad New Year!

Joy, O joy, be-yond all glad-ness, Christ has done a-way with sad-ness!

Hence, all sor-row and re-pin-ing, for the Son of Grace is shin-ing!

January 2 Wise Men, They Came to Look

TEXT: Christopher Idle ‖ b. September 11, 1938, Kent, England

Christopher Idle is a modern, living composer. Without the archaic language of earlier carols, this text maintains the quality of poetry that places it in the literature of Wesley or Watts. With degrees from Oxford and Clifton Theological College, Idle was ordained in the Church of England in 1963. He served seven different parishes while teaching, writing hymns, books, and many periodicals. He is credited with over 300 hymns.

Do an internet search of "Mary of the Incarnation" by Christopher Idle (Hope Publishing). Though not a Christmas hymn, it is about Mary the mother of Jesus, and the artistry of his hymn poetry is evident. Three stanzas start with "Mary of the incarnation," "Mary of the crucifixion," and "Mary of the resurrection." Read and perhaps sing this unique hymn. You can sing it to the melody of ODE TO JOY.

TUNE: Georg Neumark ‖ b. March 16,1621, Langensalza, Germany
d. July 8, 1681, Weimar, Germany

Combining a modern poem with an ancient tune brings dignity and beauty to both. WER NUR DEN LIEBEN GOTT is most commonly known for the text, "If Thou but Suffer God to Guide Thee." Georg Neumark was known as a writer and not a musician. The tune gained fame because of its marriage to the text that he called his "hymn of consolation, when in 1646, through a dreadful fire I came to my last farthing."[48] J. S. Bach based a cantata on the tune and text, and the tune is said to have been used with over 400 hymn texts.

As you sing this hymn . . . you gain some sanctified imagination of insight into the mind of the wise men. Each stanza gives a picture of the historical event combined with an application of how you can learn from their experience. While we may consider ourselves modern "wise men," true wisdom comes from above. While we may be aliens and without fame, God has found us, and He knows our names. While we may look for splendor and a Messiah for our lives, only Jesus gives joy for each day, songs for each night, and light for our paths. While we may offer gifts and think we can give to God, the truth is that His gift to us is far, far greater. He comes incarnate into our lives, making us a Bethlehem.

First Corinthians 2:9 exclaims, "What no eye has seen, nor ear heard, nor the heart of man imagined, what God has prepared for those who love him." We consider through these carols the beginning of the story—Jesus' brief journey to earth. But our own experience with God is only a beginning as well. Our imaginations cannot comprehend the story yet to unfold. You are on a journey—like the wise men—in great anticipation of meeting and worshiping your King. But what will unfold before you is beyond all dreams or imaginings.

Wise Men, They Came to Look

39

Wise men from the east came to Jerusalem, saying,
"Where is he who has been born king of the Jews?"

MATTHEW 2:1−2

WER NUR DEN LIEBEN GOTT
Text: Christopher Idle
Music: Georg Neumark

1. Wise men, they came to look for wis-dom,
   finding One wis-er than they knew;
   rich men they met with One yet rich-er,
   King of the kings, they knelt to You:
   Je-sus, our wis-dom from a-bove,
   wealth and re-demp-tion, life and love.

2. Pil-grims they were, from un-known coun-tries,
   search-ing for One who knows the world;
   lost are their names, and strange their jour-neys,
   famed is their zeal to find the Child:
   Je-sus, in You the lost are claimed,
   al-iens are found, and known, and named.

3. Ma-gi, they stooped to see Your splen-dor,
   led by a star to light su-preme;
   prom-ised Mes-si-ah, Lord e-ter-nal,
   glo-ry and peace are in Your name.
   Joy of each day, our Song by night,
   shine on our path Your ho-ly light.

4. Guests of their God, they o-pened trea-sures,
   in-cense and gold and sol-emn myrrh;
   wel-com-ing One too young to ques-tion
   how came these gifts, and what they were.
   Gift be-yond price of gold or gem,
   make a-mong us Your Beth-le-hem.

103

January 3   We Three Kings

TEXT AND TUNE: John H. Hopkins Jr. || b. October 28, 1820, Pittsburgh, Pennsylvania
                                          d. August 14, 1891, Hudson, New York

John Hopkins was a multitalented individual in both the arts and theology. He spent time as a journalist, and then considered law. Hopkins graduated from General Theological Seminary of the Episcopal Church in 1850 and served as the first church music instructor. He became a member of the New York Ecclesiological Society and used his talents to design stained-glass windows and church ornaments while also composing hymns. Hopkins never married and had a family, but he loved his nieces and nephews dearly. In 1857, he wrote a song for them as an Epiphany gift. Imagining what it might have been like to be a visitor from the East, he told a story in the first-person voice of the three kings. As early as the second century, Tertullian had called them kings, saying they fulfilled Isaiah's prophecy, "Nations shall come to your light, and kings to the brightness of your rising" (Isa. 60:3). Although the Scriptures do not specify, tradition has numbered them as three because of the three separate gifts. But the number of visitors could have been more.

Hopkins created the tune, named KINGS OF ORIENT, in a lilting rhythm that imitates the swaying gait of camels. The stanzas tell the story in a minor key, giving it solemnity and a touch of Middle Eastern flavor. (Orient should not be mistaken for East Asia or China but rather Persia, known today as Iran.) At the repeating refrain, the music changes to the relative major key as we joy in the wonder of the star that led them.

As you sing this hymn . . . you are singing a story of joyful worship. What is the purpose of this story that only the gospel of Matthew gives to us? It focuses on two things: the desire of these men to find the prophesied King and their understanding that when they found Him, He was to be worshiped and honored with gifts. Read the entire Matthew account found in "Christmas in the Bible," #27–30. Some translations describe the reaction of the travelers upon seeing the Child as, "they fell down," literally prostrating themselves. Further, Matthew adds powerful adjectives. Their worship was not just with joy, but with *great* joy. They didn't just rejoice; they did so *exceedingly*. Can you even imagine this scene?

The carol interprets the significance of their gifts: precious gold that you would give a king as you submit to his reign; frankincense, a precious incense or perfume used to honor a deity; and myrrh, a rare and strong perfume that was particularly significant as a burial ointment to counter the smell of death. Was the latter a prophetic gift regarding the future of this King? These gifts serve as symbols of our heart-gifts of worship. Christmas gifts remain a holiday custom, but at some point, our gifts changed from gifts to God into gifts to one another. Giving one another gifts at Christmas is not wrong. But the question should be asked, what are you giving to God in your Christmas worship? Most important, do you look as did the wise men for the glory of God revealed—perhaps not by a star, but in the wonder and glory of God's redemptive work in your life? Then do you follow the example of these wise men to fall down, submitting your allegiance and obedience to the Christ of Bethlehem? The carol says His light is *still* leading and *still* proceeding to guide us to the Perfect Light. Let us follow the wise men's example.

We Three Kings

40

And going into the house, they saw the child with Mary his mother,
and they fell down and worshiped him.
Then, opening their treasures, they offered him gifts,
gold and frankincense and myrrh.

MATTHEW 2:11

KINGS OF ORIENT
Text: J. H. Hopkins Jr.
Music: J. H. Hopkins Jr.

1. We three kings of Or - i - ent are,   bear - ing gifts we trav - erse a - far,
2. Born a King on Beth - le - hem's plain, gold I bring to crown Him a - gain,
3. Frank - in - cense to   of - fer have I,   in - cense owns a   De - i - ty nigh;
4. Myrrh is mine, its bit - ter per - fume breathes a life of gath - er - ing gloom,
5. Glo - rious now be - hold Him a - rise, King and God and Sac - ri - fice;

field   and foun - tain, moor and moun - tain, fol - low - ing yon - der   star.
King   for - ev - er, ceas - ing nev - er   o - ver us all   to   reign.
prayer and prais - ing, voi - ces rais - ing, wor - ship - ing God on   high.
Sor - rowing, sigh - ing, bleed - ing, dy - ing, sealed in the stone - cold tomb.
Al - le - lu - ia, Al - le - lu - ia! Earth__ to heav'n re - plies.

O,___   star of won - der, star of night,   star with roy - al beau - ty bright.

West - ward lead - ing, still pro - ceed - ing, guide us to   thy per - fect light.

January 4   Brightest and Best of the Stars of the Morning

TEXT: Reginald Heber ‖ b. April 21, 1783, Cheshire, England
d. April 3, 1826, Trichinopoly, India

Reginald Heber was born into an aristocratic Yorkshire family. He could read the Bible fluently at age five and astonished even his parents with his understanding of its content. He won a prize for a poem about Palestine at age seventeen. Educated at Oxford University and surrounded by the beautiful writings of Shelley, Keats, and Byron, Heber wrote fifty-seven poems, most of which remain in print today. As a young man, Heber's devotion to God developed into a great passion for missions. His hymn "From Greenland's Icy Mountains" was an expression of this burden. At age forty, he moved to India where he became the Anglican Bishop of Calcutta (Kolkata). After only two years, he was overcome by heat stroke and unexpectantly died at age forty-two. His widow discovered his hymns in a trunk and compiled them into a book. Among them was "Holy, Holy, Holy" and this hymn, "Brightest and Best of the Stars of the Morning."

TUNE: James P. Harding ‖ b. May 19, 1890, London, England
d. February 21, 1911, London, England

Little is known about James Harding except that he was the choir director of St. Andrew's Church in Islington, London, for thirty-five years. He also served as a civil servant for London. He composed choral anthems, for which the tune MORNING STAR was created. Its dignity has made this a much-loved hymn and tune.

*As you sing this hymn . . .*you are fully entering into the meaning of the word Epiphany. Although this text never uses the term wise men, it is as if we are those who followed the brightest star in the sky to find the King whom it announced. Revelation 22:16 refers to Jesus as the "bright morning star." As He illuminates our earthly pilgrimage, we recognize Him as "Maker [Creator] and Monarch and Savior of all!" Such a revelation begs the question, "What shall we offer Him?" Surely we cannot worship empty-handed. Are there jewels or pearls or any gifts of gold worthy of this King? Does the story of the wise men's offerings provide a pattern of how we must worship?

Heber understood that we do not "buy" this King's favor with treasures of gifts. "Vainly," he says, would we attempt to win God's favor by material gifts or offerings. Not even being good enough, going to church enough, or reading our Bible enough—no actions of ours will win our soul's release from the slavery of sin. The riches God wants from us are our hearts' adoration. He seeks our submission to His gift of grace in forgiveness. Although Heber grew up among earthly riches, no doubt it was in the poverty of Calcutta that he saw the prayers of the poor as the greatest thing God seeks. "God be merciful to me a sinner" must be our Epiphany prayer.

Brightest and Best of the Stars of the Morning

41

*The people who walked in darkness
have seen a great light.*

ISAIAH 9:2

Text: Reginald Heber
Music: James P. Harding

1. Bright - est and best of the stars__ of the morn - ing,
2. Cold on His cra - dle the dew - drops are shin - ing,
3. What shall we give Him, in cost - ly de - vo - tion?
4. Vain - ly we of - fer each lav - ish ob - la - tion,

dawn on our dark - ness and come__ to our aid;
low lies His head with the beasts__ of the stall;
Shall we bring in - cense and of - erings di - vine,
vain - ly with gifts would His fa - vor se - cure;

star of the east, the ho - ri - zon a - dorn - ing,
An - gels a - dore Him in slum - ber re - clin - ing,
gems of the moun - tain and pearls__ of the o - cean,
rich - er by far is the heart's ad - o - ra - tion,

guide where our in - fant Re - deem - er is laid.
Mak - er and Mon - arch and Sav - ior of all!
myrrh from the for - est or gold__ from the mine?
dear - er to God are the prayers of the poor.*

*Repeat Stanza 1

January 5   Thou Didst Leave Thy Throne

TEXT: Emily S. Elliott || b. July 22, 1836, Sussex, England
d. August 3, 1897, London, England

Emily Elliott was the daughter of a pastor, Edward Bishop Elliott of St. Mark's Church in Brighton, England. Her aunt was Charlotte Elliott, who wrote the popular hymn, "Just as I Am." Emily Elliott wrote numerous hymns for her father's church, including a collection of seventy hymns and poems called *Chimes of Consecration*. A subsequent book, *Chimes for Daily Service*, contained seventy-one hymns. Elliott also published a large-print hymn book called *Under the Pillow* for use in nursing homes.

TUNE: Timothy R. Matthews || b. November 4, 1826, Colmworth, England
d. January 5, 1910, Lincolnshire, England

Timothy Matthews was also the child of an English pastor who, after studying at Cambridge, became the Canon of St. George's Chapel, Windsor Castle. Matthews composed "Morning and Evening Services" and chants and responses, and he earned a reputation for simple but effective hymn tunes, writing over a hundred. A man once requested six tunes from him for a children's hymnal, and Matthews completed them within a day.

As you sing this hymn . . . you are engaged in a conversation with Jesus. You have read His story in Luke 2:7, which tells that Mary "gave birth to her firstborn son and wrapped him in swaddling cloths and laid him in a manger, because there was no place for them in the inn." Why would God have permitted such an inhospitable, perhaps unsanitary, and uncommon place for His Son to be born? Could there be any greater contrast between the glories of heaven and a stable on earth? No room for the Messiah and Creator of the universe? We've heard this all our lives, but will it ever cease to amaze us?

What is the significance of this lowly birthplace? The nineteenth-century English preacher, Charles Spurgeon, offers the following reasons: 1) to clearly show His humiliation—"A man of sorrows and acquainted with grief" began at birth. 2) "By being in a manger, *he was declared to be the king of the poor*." No wonder the shepherds felt comfortable coming in to see Him. 3) "Being laid in a manger, he did . . . *give an invitation to the most humble to come to him*." 4) This place was open and free to everyone—no standard of worth or rite of passage. There may not even have been a door.[49]

Ironically, continues Spurgeon, there were other places, both then and now, that have no room for Christ. But He "stands at the door and knocks" (Rev. 3:20). So the question remains: Is there room in your heart for Him? This carol offers you the opportunity to repeatedly affirm, "Come to my heart, Lord Jesus. There is room in my heart for Thee." And His promise is, "if you open the door, I will come in" (v. 20).

But the final stanza changes the location. One day, Jesus will invite His own into His home for eternity. He will say, "Yes, there is room!" What else can we say but "my heart will rejoice when you call me home, Lord Jesus"? Can you sing this confidently? Trust His promises today.

Thou Didst Leave Thy Throne

42

I pray that out of his glorious riches he may strengthen you
with power through his Spirit in your inner being,
so that Christ may dwell in your hearts through faith.

EPHESIANS 3:16–17 NIV

MARGARET
Text: Emily S. Elliott
Music: Timothy R. Matthews

1. Thou didst leave Thy___ throne and Thy king - ly crown when Thou
2. Heav-en's arch - es___ rang and the an - gels sang, pro -
3. Thou___ cam - est, O Lord, with the liv - ing word that should
4. When the heav - ens shall ring, and the an - gels sing, at Thy

1. cam - est to earth for___ me; but in Beth - le - hem's home was there
2. claim-ing Thy roy - al de - gree; but of low - ly___ birth Thou didst
3. set Thy_ peo - ple___ free; but with mock - ing___ scorn, and with
4. com - ing to vic - to - ry. let Thy voice call me home, say - ing,

1. found no___ room for Thy ho - ly na - tiv - i - ty.
2. come to___ earth, and in great hu - mil - i - ty.
3. crown of___ thorn, they_ bore Thee to Cal - va - ry.
4. "Yet there is room, there is room at My side for thee."

1. O come to my heart, Lord Je - sus, there is room in my heart for_ Thee!
2. O come to my heart, Lord Je - sus, there is room in my heart for_ Thee!
3. O come to my heart, Lord Je - sus, there is room in my heart for_ Thee!
4. My heart shall re - joice, Lord Je - sus, when Thou com-est and call-est for me!

January 6 In the Bleak Midwinter

TEXT: Christina G. Rossetti ‖ b. December 5, 1830, London, England
d. December 29, 1894, Bloomsbury, England

Born into a gifted family of poets and artists, Christina Rossetti was a leading English poet of the Victorian era and was compared favorably with her contemporary, the famous poet Elizabeth Barrett Browning. Rossetti's father emigrated from Italy in 1824 and became a professor at King's College. Her mother homeschooled Rossetti and her two sisters and brother. Their home education included *The Pilgrim's Progress* and the works of St. Augustine. Of her voluminous output of romantic, devotional, and children's poetry, Rossetti is most known today for two poems that have been set to music, "Love Came Down at Christmas" and "In the Bleak Midwinter."

TUNE: Gustav T. Holst ‖ b. September 21, 1874, Cheltham, England
d. May 25, 1934, London, England

One of England's most famous nineteenth century composers, Gustav Holst is best known for his orchestral suite, *The Planets*. A teacher and professional trombonist, he wrote dozens of compositions for almost every musical medium. Biographer Michael Short wrote, "many people who may never hear any of Holst's major works . . . have nevertheless derived great pleasure from hearing or singing such small masterpieces as the carol, 'In the Bleak Midwinter.'"[50] The great hymn "O God Beyond All Praising" is a tune derived from "Jupiter" from *The Planets*. Since "In the Bleak Midwinter" is irregular in meter, it demands care to follow the several extra melody notes to be sung or ignored to match all the syllables.

As you sing this hymn . . . you may wonder why this carol was chosen to end these forty-three hymns and the Epiphany section. This carol summarizes the Christmas story with four vivid pictures: the place, the prophecy, the adoration, and our response. The first stanza appears to be in error as to the place, for Bethlehem would not have snowy, cold winters—or even the certainty that Jesus' birth was in winter. But allegorically, whether or not Rossetti meant this, it is certainly a "bleak" picture of the cold and hostile world—a world without hope—into which Jesus came. We could even say the "snow on snow on snow" was the growing hostility that led Him to death on a cross.

The second stanza alludes to the first coming where Jesus did not need a palace or throne. A stable was "sufficient." But Christ's second coming, "when He comes to reign," prophesies the destruction of heaven and earth as described in 2 Peter 3:10, "But the day of the Lord will come like a thief. The heavens will disappear with a roar; the elements will be destroyed by fire, and the earth and everything in it will be laid bare" (NIV). Rossetti's third stanza describes the adoration that began in Bethlehem when the angels gathered in worship. How tenderly she describes Mary's worship, "with a kiss." This is not worship devoid of emotion, and neither should ours be. The fourth stanza brings us to the close of this Christmas season with a question: How do we respond? We acknowledge we are incapable of any worthy gift. But God gives us a heart to know Him (Jer. 24:7). In return, we give Him our hearts. On this last day of the season, make this your purposeful and glad response. If you have never declared Jesus as your Lord and Savior; there is no better time than now.

In the Bleak Midwinter

43

I will give them a heart to know that I am the LORD,
and they shall be my people and I will be their God,
for they shall return to me with their whole heart.

JEREMIAH 24:7

CRANHAM
Text: Christina G. Rossetti
Music: Gustav T. Holst

1. In the bleak mid - win - ter, frost - y wind made moan,
2. Our God heav'n can - not hold him, nor___ earth sus - tain.
3. An - gels and arch - an - gels may have gath-ered there,
4. What___ can I give Him, poor___ as I am?

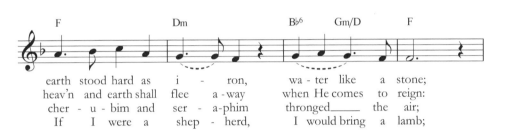

earth stood hard as i - ron, wa - ter like a stone;
heav'n and earth shall flee a - way when He comes to reign:
cher - u - bim and ser - a-phim thronged___ the air;
If I were a shep - herd, I would bring a lamb;

snow had fall - en snow on snow, snow___ on___ snow,
in the bleak mid - win - ter a sta - ble place suf - ficed
but His moth - er on___ ly, in her maid - en bliss,
if I were a wise___ man, I would do my part;

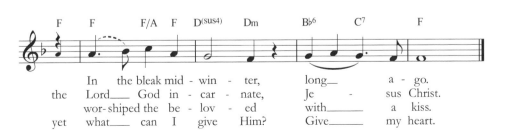

In the bleak mid - win - ter, long___ a - go.
the Lord___ God in - car - nate, Je - sus Christ.
wor - shiped the be - lov - ed with___ a kiss.
yet what___ can I give Him? Give___ my heart.

Christmas in the Bible

Although the word "Christmas" is not in the Bible, the story of Christmas is found throughout. The word "holiday" comes from the words "holy day,"[51] which have their foundation in the holy events of the incarnation, the death, and resurrection of Christ. The following Scriptures are provided for private reading and meditation, with many referenced in the "As you sing this hymn" sections. For use as public reading during times of worship, the passages are set in paragraphs with plain and bold fonts to more easily enable antiphonal reading—back and forth between two readers or groups of readers.

From the Old Testament

1. Therefore the Lord himself will give you a sign. Behold, the virgin shall conceive and bear a son, and shall call his name Immanuel. (Isa. 7:14)

2. **The people who walked in darkness have seen a great light; those who dwelt in a land of deep darkness, on them has light shone. . . . ⁶ For to us a child is born, to us a son is given; and the government shall be upon his shoulder, and his name shall be called Wonderful Counselor, Mighty God, Everlasting Father, Prince of Peace. ⁷ Of the increase of his government and of peace there will be no end, on the throne of David and over his kingdom, to establish it and to uphold it with justice and with righteousness from this time forth and forevermore. The zeal of the LORD of hosts will do this. (Isa. 9:2, 6–7)**

3. There shall come forth a shoot from the stump of Jesse, and a branch from his roots shall bear fruit. . . . ¹⁰ In that day the root of Jesse, who shall stand as a signal for the peoples—of him shall the nations inquire, and his resting place shall be glorious. (Isa. 11:1, 10)

4. **"Comfort, comfort my people," says your God. ² Speak tenderly to Jerusalem, and cry to her that her warfare is ended, that her iniquity is**

pardoned, that she has received from the LORD's hand double for all her sins. ³ A voice cries: "In the wilderness prepare the way of the LORD; make straight in the desert a highway for our God. ⁴ Every valley shall be lifted up, and every mountain and hill be made low; the uneven ground shall become level, and the rough places a plain. ⁵ And the glory of the LORD shall be revealed, and all flesh shall see it together, for the mouth of the LORD has spoken." (Isa. 40:1–5)

5. Arise, shine, for your light has come, and the glory of the LORD has risen upon you. ² For behold, darkness shall cover the earth, and thick darkness the peoples; but the LORD will arise upon you, and his glory will be seen upon you. ³ And nations shall come to your light, and kings to the brightness of your rising. . . . ⁶ A multitude of camels shall cover you, the young camels of Midian and Ephah; all those from Sheba shall come. They shall bring gold and frankincense, and shall bring good news, the praises of the LORD. (Isa. 60:1–3, 6)

6. "Behold, the days are coming, declares the LORD, when I will raise up for David a righteous Branch, and he shall reign as king and deal wisely, and shall execute justice and righteousness in the land." (Jer. 23:5)

7. When Israel was a child, I loved him, and out of Egypt I called my son. (Hosea 11:1)

8. But you, O Bethlehem Ephrathah, who are too little to be among the clans of Judah, from you shall come forth for me one who is to be ruler in Israel, whose coming forth is from of old, from ancient days. . . . ⁴ And he shall stand and shepherd his flock in the strength of the LORD, in the majesty of the name of the LORD his God. And they shall dwell secure, for now he shall be great to the ends of the earth. ⁵ And he shall be their peace. (Micah 5:2, 4–5a)

From the Gospels

9. ¹⁸ Now the birth of Jesus Christ took place in this way. When his mother Mary had been betrothed to Joseph, before they came together she was found to be with child from the Holy Spirit. ¹⁹ And her husband Joseph, being a just man and unwilling to put her to shame, resolved to divorce her quietly.

10. ²⁰ But as he considered these things, behold, an angel of the Lord appeared to him in a dream, saying, "Joseph, son of David, do not fear to

take Mary as your wife, for that which is conceived in her is from the Holy Spirit. [21] She will bear a son, and you shall call his name Jesus, for he will save his people from their sins."

11. [22] All this took place to fulfill what the Lord had spoken by the prophet:

12. [23] "Behold, the virgin shall conceive and bear a son, and they shall call his name Immanuel" (which means, God with us). [24] When Joseph woke from sleep, he did as the angel of the Lord commanded him: he took his wife, [25] but knew her not until she had given birth to a son. And he called his name Jesus. (Matt. 1:18–25)

13. [26] In the sixth month the angel Gabriel was sent from God to a city of Galilee named Nazareth, [27] to a virgin betrothed to a man whose name was Joseph, of the house of David. And the virgin's name was Mary. [28] And he came to her and said, "Greetings, O favored one, the Lord is with you!" [29] But she was greatly troubled at the saying, and tried to discern what sort of greeting this might be. [30] And the angel said to her,

14. "Do not be afraid, Mary, for you have found favor with God. [31] And behold, you will conceive in your womb and bear a son, and you shall call his name Jesus. [32] He will be great and will be called the Son of the Most High. And the Lord God will give to him the throne of his father David, [33] and he will reign over the house of Jacob forever, and of his kingdom there will be no end."

15. [34] And Mary said to the angel, "How will this be, since I am a virgin?"

16. [35] And the angel answered her, "The Holy Spirit will come upon you, and the power of the Most High will overshadow you; therefore the child to be born will be called holy—the Son of God. [36] And behold, your relative Elizabeth in her old age has also conceived a son, and this is the sixth month with her who was called barren. [37] For nothing will be impossible with God."

17. [38] And Mary said, "Behold, I am the servant of the Lord; let it be to me according to your word." And the angel departed from her. (Luke 1:26–38)

18. [39] In those days Mary arose and went with haste into the hill country, to a town in Judah, [40] and she entered the house of Zechariah and greeted Elizabeth. [41] And when Elizabeth heard the greeting of Mary, the baby leaped in her womb. And Elizabeth was filled with the Holy Spirit, [42] and

she exclaimed with a loud cry, "Blessed are you among women, and blessed is the fruit of your womb!

19. [43] And why is this granted to me that the mother of my Lord should come to me? [44] For behold, when the sound of your greeting came to my ears, the baby in my womb leaped for joy. [45] And blessed is she who believed that there would be a fulfillment of what was spoken to her from the Lord."

20. [46] And Mary said, "My soul magnifies the Lord, [47] and my spirit rejoices in God my Savior, [48] for he has looked on the humble estate of his servant. For behold, from now on all generations will call me blessed; [49] for he who is mighty has done great things for me, and holy is his name. [50] And his mercy is for those who fear him from generation to generation. [51] He has shown strength with his arm; he has scattered the proud in the thoughts of their hearts; [52] he has brought down the mighty from their thrones and exalted those of humble estate; [53] he has filled the hungry with good things, and the rich he has sent away empty. [54] He has helped his servant Israel, in remembrance of his mercy, [55] as he spoke to our fathers, to Abraham and to his offspring forever."

21. [56] And Mary remained with her about three months and returned to her home. (Luke 1:39–56)

22. In those days a decree went out from Caesar Augustus that all the world should be registered. [2] This was the first registration when Quirinius was governor of Syria. [3] And all went to be registered, each to his own town.

23. [4] And Joseph also went up from Galilee, from the town of Nazareth, to Judea, to the city of David, which is called Bethlehem, because he was of the house and lineage of David, [5] to be registered with Mary, his betrothed, who was with child. [6] And while they were there, the time came for her to give birth. [7] And she gave birth to her firstborn son and wrapped him in swaddling cloths and laid him in a manger, because there was no place for them in the inn.

24. [8] And in the same region there were shepherds out in the field, keeping watch over their flock by night. [9] And an angel of the Lord appeared to them, and the glory of the Lord shone around them, and they were filled with great fear. [10] And the angel said to them, "Fear not, for behold, I bring you good news of great joy that will be for all the people. [11] For unto you is born this day in the city of David a Savior, who is Christ the Lord. [12] And

this will be a sign for you: you will find a baby wrapped in swaddling cloths and lying in a manger."

25. [13] And suddenly there was with the angel a multitude of the heavenly host praising God and saying, [14] "Glory to God in the highest, and on earth peace among those with whom he is pleased!"

26. [15] When the angels went away from them into heaven, the shepherds said to one another, "Let us go over to Bethlehem and see this thing that has happened, which the Lord has made known to us." [16] And they went with haste and found Mary and Joseph, and the baby lying in a manger. [17] And when they saw it, they made known the saying that had been told them concerning this child. [18] And all who heard it wondered at what the shepherds told them. [19] But Mary treasured up all these things, pondering them in her heart. [20] And the shepherds returned, glorifying and praising God for all they had heard and seen, as it had been told them. (Luke 2:1–20)

27. Now after Jesus was born in Bethlehem of Judea in the days of Herod the king, behold, wise men from the east came to Jerusalem, [2] saying, "Where is he who has been born king of the Jews? For we saw his star when it rose and have come to worship him."

28. [3] When Herod the king heard this, he was troubled, and all Jerusalem with him; [4] and assembling all the chief priests and scribes of the people, he inquired of them where the Christ was to be born. [5] They told him, "In Bethlehem of Judea, for so it is written by the prophet: [6] "'And you, O Bethlehem, in the land of Judah, are by no means least among the rulers of Judah; for from you shall come a ruler who will shepherd my people Israel.'"

29. [7] Then Herod summoned the wise men secretly and ascertained from them what time the star had appeared. [8] And he sent them to Bethlehem, saying, "Go and search diligently for the child, and when you have found him, bring me word, that I too may come and worship him."

30. [9] After listening to the king, they went on their way. And behold, the star that they had seen when it rose went before them until it came to rest over the place where the child was. [10] When they saw the star, they rejoiced exceedingly with great joy. [11] And going into the house, they saw the child with Mary his mother, and they fell down and worshiped him. Then, opening their treasures, they offered him gifts, gold and frankincense

and myrrh. [12] And being warned in a dream not to return to Herod, they departed to their own country by another way. (Matt. 2:1–12)

31. The true light, which gives light to everyone, was coming into the world. [10] He was in the world, and the world was made through him, yet the world did not know him. [11] He came to his own, and his own people did not receive him. [12] But to all who did receive him, who believed in his name, he gave the right to become children of God, [13] who were born, not of blood nor of the will of the flesh nor of the will of man, but of God. [14] And the Word became flesh and dwelt among us, and we have seen his glory, glory as of the only Son from the Father, full of grace and truth. (John 1:9–14)

32. Now there was a man of the Pharisees named Nicodemus, a ruler of the Jews. [2] This man came to Jesus by night and said to him, "Rabbi, we know that you are a teacher come from God, for no one can do these signs that you do unless God is with him."

33. [3] Jesus answered him, "Truly, truly, I say to you, unless one is born again he cannot see the kingdom of God."

34. [4] Nicodemus said to him, "How can a man be born when he is old? Can he enter a second time into his mother's womb and be born?"

35. [5] Jesus answered, "Truly, truly, I say to you, unless one is born of water and the Spirit, he cannot enter the kingdom of God. [6] That which is born of the flesh is flesh, and that which is born of the Spirit is spirit. [7] Do not marvel that I said to you, 'You must be born again.' [8] The wind blows where it wishes, and you hear its sound, but you do not know where it comes from or where it goes. So it is with everyone who is born of the Spirit." (John 3:1–8)

36. "For God so loved the world, that he gave his only Son, that whoever believes in him should not perish but have eternal life. [17] For God did not send his Son into the world to condemn the world, but in order that the world might be saved through him." (John 3:16–17)

From the Epistles

37. Great indeed, we confess, is the mystery of godliness: He was manifested in the flesh, vindicated by the Spirit, seen by angels, proclaimed among the nations, believed on in the world, taken up in glory. (1 Tim. 3:16)

38. But when the fullness of time had come, God sent forth his Son, born of woman, born under the law, [5] to redeem those who were under the law, so that we might receive adoption as sons. [6] And because you are sons, God has sent the Spirit of his Son into our hearts, crying, "Abba! Father!" [7] So you are no longer a slave, but a son, and if a son, then an heir through God. (Gal. 4:4–7)

39. Have this mind among yourselves, which is yours in Christ Jesus, [6] who, though he was in the form of God, did not count equality with God a thing to be grasped, [7] but emptied himself, by taking the form of a servant, being born in the likeness of men. [8] And being found in human form, he humbled himself by becoming obedient to the point of death, even death on a cross. [9] Therefore God has highly exalted him and bestowed on him the name that is above every name, [10] so that at the name of Jesus every knee should bow, in heaven and on earth and under the earth, [11] and every tongue confess that Jesus Christ is Lord, to the glory of God the Father. (Phil. 2:5–11)

40. Then I heard what seemed to be the voice of a great multitude, like the roar of many waters and like the sound of mighty peals of thunder, crying out, "Hallelujah! For the Lord our God the Almighty reigns. [7] Let us rejoice and exult and give him the glory, for the marriage of the Lamb has come, and his Bride has made herself ready. . . . [16] On his robe and on his thigh he has a name written, King of kings and Lord of lords." (Rev. 19: 6–7, 16)

COPYRIGHT HOLDERS | Various copyright holders and publishers have granted permission for inclusion of their copyrighted material in *Hosanna in Excelsis*. These are listed below. If you are interested in using or reproducing any of this copyrighted material (words or music), please seek permission from the copyright holder.

Alphabetical Index of Hymns

Acknowledgments

Although we grew up in different parts of the country and did not meet until college, we both grew up in families that sang hymns at church and at home. When on road trips, both of us recall singing every hymn we could remember, starting with each letter of the alphabet! This book is perhaps more than anything a heritage of parents who taught us to love hymns. Interestingly, Dave's parents both attended Moody Bible Institute, and he grew up reading many books from Moody Publishers.

We have passed a tradition of hymn singing on to our four grown children, and today they all take their families to churches where hymns are the primary music for worship. Our oldest son, Jonathan Leeman, is an author and editor for 9 Marks Ministry in Washington, DC. With a PhD in theology, he helped greatly in checking our theology, offering suggestions in numerous places— particularly in the explanations of Advent, the Nativity, and Epiphany.

We are so grateful for Andrew Wolgemuth of Wolgemuth and Associates, who caught our vision for this book and introduced us to Moody Publishers and acquiring editor Amy Simpson. She and the Moody team shared our vision for helping the Christian world to retain and review the great hymns and carols of Christmas. Amy has shepherded us through this process like a friend, making this a wonderful experience.

About the Authors

David and Barbara Leeman are both graduates of Biola University School of Music. Barbara also earned a teacher's credential from the University of Oregon, and Dave earned a master's degree in Choral Conducting from California State University in Fullerton. He is now retired after more than forty-three years of serving as minister of music and worship at churches in California, Oregon, Illinois, and Texas. Barbara has taught private piano and music education for early childhood through middle school. She retired after twenty-three years as the music teacher at Providence Christian School of Texas. They continue to serve as non-paid musicians in the church they attend. Dave and Barbara were both raised in Christian homes where hymnody was loved. They remember car trips where the family often sang hymns together. In 2014, they produced a similar hymnal, but designed for students, entitled *Hosanna, Loud Hosannas*. The Christmas collection, *Hosanna in Excelsis*, is only one of a future set of similar books designed to preserve the best of hymns along with their stories and devotional messages.

Notes

1. G. F. Handel, *Messiah*, "Hallelujah Chorus."

2. Merriam-Webster, s.v. "carol," last updated June 15, 2020, https://www.merriam-webster.com/dictionary/carol.

3. Michelle Blake, *The Tentmaker* (New York: Penguin, 2000), 155.

4. Robert Herrick, "A Christmas Carol Sung to the King in the Presence at Whitehall," in *A Wreath of Christmas Carols and Poems*, chosen and edited with notes by William Andrews (Hull, England: J. R. Tutin, 1906), 38–39.

5. "Louis Bourgeois (composer)," Wikipedia, last edited January 30, 2020, https://en.wikipedia.org/wiki/Louis_Bourgeois_(composer).

6. Mark Dever, *The Message of the Old Testament* (Wheaton, IL: Crossway Books, 2006), 585.

7. Scotty Smith, "A Prayer for the First Sunday of Advent," The Gospel Coalition, December 1, 2013, https://www.thegospelcoalition.org/blogs/scotty-smith/a-prayer-for-the-first-sunday-of-advent-3/.

8. Skip Moen, "Comfort," Hebrew Word Study, January 20, 2003, https://www.skipmoen.com/2003/01/comfort.

9. John Julian, *Dictionary of Hymnology* (New York: Dover Publications, 1957), 1:1277.

10. J. C. Ryle, "J. C. Ryle's Expository Thoughts on the Gospels: Matthew 1," Studylight.org, https://www.studylight.org/commentaries/ryl/matthew-1.html.

11. John Piper, "O Come, O Come Emmanuel," Desiring God, December 13, 2015, https://www.desiringgod.org/articles/o-come-o-come-emmanuel.

12. Wikipedia; Wikipedia's "Hyfrydol" entry, https://findwords.info/term/hyfrydol.

13. Charles Spurgeon, *Morning and Evening* (Peabody, MA: Hendrickson Publishers, 1995), 78.

14. Kevin DeYoung, "Of the Father's Love Begotton," The Gospel Coalition (Blog), December 11, 2015, https://www.thegospelcoalition.org/blogs/kevin-deyoung/of-the-fathers-love-begotten-4.

15. Phillip Doddridge, *The Works of Rev. P. Doddridge*, vol. 1 (Leeds, England: E. Baines, 1802), 20.

16. Michael Green, *The Truth of God Incarnate* (London: Hodder and Stoughton, 1977), 36.

17. C. S. Lewis, "One Grand Miracle," *God in the Dock: Essays on Theology and Ethics* (Grand Rapids, MI: Eerdmans, 2002), 9.

18. John Milton "On the Morning of Christ's Nativity," composed 1629, in *Paradise Lost and Other Poems of John Milton*, ed. Maurice Kelley (New York: Walter J. Black, 1943), 6–9.

19. James Montgomery, *Sacred Poems and Hymns* (New York: D. Appleton and Co., 1854), No. CCXXXIX, 239–40.

20. "Welkin," Merriam-Webster online, https://www.merriam-webster.com/dictionary/welkin.

21. Carl Schalk, "Hymn Writer Jaroslav Vajda Dies," *The LCMS Reporter*, May 22, 2008.

22. David Strand, "Now the Poet," *The Lutheran Witness*, March 1996.

23. "Edmond Hamilton Sears," Dictionary of Unitarian and Universalist Biography, https://uudb.org/articles/edmundhamiltonsears.html.

24. Edmond H. Sears, *Sermons and Songs of the Christian Life,* https://www.umcdiscipleship.org/resources/history-of-hymns-it-came-upon-a-midnight-clear.

25. John M. Mulder, F. Morgan Roberts, *Twenty-Eight Carols to Sing at Christmas* (Eugene, OR: Cascade Books, 2015), 117.

26. John MacArthur, "We Beheld His Glory," sermon, Grace to You, December 25, 2011, https://www.gty.org/library/sermons-library/90-423/we-beheld-his-glory.

27. Public address at the Sing 2019 Conference, Nashville, TN, August 2019.

28. Charles H. Spurgeon, *Morning and Evening* (Peabody, MA: Hendrickson Publishers, Inc., 1995), 54.

29. David Mathis, "What Child is This?: Poverty, Not a Palace, for the Greatest King," December 6, 2015, https://www.desiringgod.org/articles/what-child-is-this.

30. Richard Philips, sermon, Second Presbyterian Church, Greenville, SC, December 24, 2017.

31. *The Hymns and Carols of Christmas,* https://www.hymnsandcarolsofchristmas.com/Hymns_and_Carols/Biographies/john_jacob_niles.htm.

32. Ligon Duncan, "Songs of Christmas," sermon, First Presbyterian Church, Jackson, MS, December 13, 2004.

33. "I Heard the Bells on Christmas Day—Hope Surfaces from Despair," New England Historical Society, Arts and Leisure, https://www.newenglandhistoricalsociety.com/heard-the-bells-christmas-day-hope-surfaces-despair/.

34. John Piper, "The Meaning of the Manger," Desiring God, November 30, 2017, https://www.desiringgod.org/articles/the-meaning-of-the-manger.

35. Some sources give his birthplace as Douai, France, or England.

36. Sheldon Vanauken, *A Severe Mercy* (New York: HarperCollins Publishers, 1980), 86.

37. Joseph Hart, "Come, Ye Sinners, Poor and Need," 1759, Timeless Truths, https://library.timelesstruths.org/music/Come_Ye_Sinners_Poor_and_Needy/.

38. John Milton "On the Morning of Christ's Nativity," composed 1629, in *Paradise Lost and Other Poems of John Milton*, ed. Maurice Kelley (New York: Walter J. Black, 1943), 5, 9.

39. Isaac Watts, quoted in Mark Galli, "Isaac Watts," *Christian History, Christianity Today*, https://www.christianitytoday.com/history/people/poets/isaac-watts.html.

40. Marshall Segal, "Joy to the World," Desiring God, December 2, 2014, https://www.desiringgod.org/articles/joy-to-the-world.

41. Stuart Townend, "Do We Really Need More Worship Songs?," October 1, 2012, https://www.stuarttownend.co.uk/do-we-really-need-more-worship-songs.

42. Antonín Dvořák, interview in *New York Herald*, May 21, 1893.

43. James Moffatt, *Handbook to the Church Hymnary* (Oxford: Oxford University Press, 1927), 318.

44. Jane Stuart Smith, Betty Carlson, *Great Christian Hymn Writers* (Wheaton, IL: Crossway, 1997), 80.

45. Ibid.

46. Elizabeth Elliott, *The Shadow of the Almighty* (New York: Harper Publishing, 1958), 53.

47. Jim Denison, "What Are God's New Year's Resolutions?," Denison Forum, December 28, 2019, https://www.denisonforum.org/resources/what-are-gods-new-years-resolutions.

48. "Neumark," Hymnary.org, https://hymnary.org/person/Neumark_GC.

49. Charles H. Spurgeon, *Spurgeon's Sermons on Jesus and the Holy Spirit* (Peabody, MA: Hendrickson Publishers, 2006), 28–31.

50. Michael Short, *Gustav Holst, The Man and His Music* (Hastings, Sussex, United Kingdom: Circaidy Gregory Press, 1990), 96.

51. Online Etymology Dictionary, s.v. "holiday (n.)," https://www.etymonline.com/word/holiday.

It's a question hundreds of pastors ask
every day: *What is the best way to grow?*

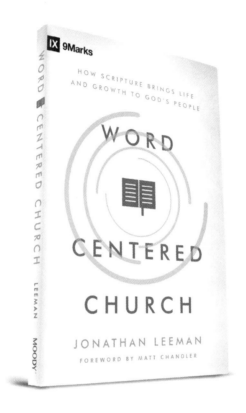

Theological and practical, *Word-Centered Church*
focuses on how the church hears, responds to,
discusses, implements, and is transformed by
Scripture. It is the ministry-model book that churches
need because it advances the model God designed.
For anyone who wants to grow or help others grow,
Word-Centered Church is indispensable.

978-0-8024-1559-2 | also available as an eBook